The Five Nights of St. Albans

THE FIVE NIGHTS

OF

ST. ALBANS.

VOL. III.

SHACKELL AND BAYLIS, JOHNSON'S-COURT, LONDON.

THE FIVE NIGHTS

· OF

ST. ALBANS.

IN THREE VOLUMES.

VOL. III.

WILLIAM BLACKWOOD, EDINBURGH; AND
T. CADELL, STRAND, LONDON.
MDCCCXXIX.

THE

FIVE NIGHTS

OF

ST. ALBANS.

CHAPTER I.

BEFORE Peverell left the mayor's, and just as he had intimated to him that they intended repeating their visit to the Abbey, that night, they were interrupted by the arrival of Giles Goosecap, the head-borough, whose face expressed, before his tongue could speak, that he had something terrible to unfold.

" Well, Giles," said his worship, " what hath befallen, that thou comest in such haste, and with so crazed a look ?"

" Beshrew me," quoth Goosecap, " I *am* amazed ; and what is more, bewildered, and what is more, astonished, and what is more than all, I am perplexed !"

" Well : — and the cause — the matter — the occasion, and moreover, the particular circumstance, of your four predicaments ?" said Peverell, humouring the amplitude of Giles's category.

" You don't know then ?— That is, you haven't been surprised, of what hath happened ? Why, the whole town is in a state of promotion, or, as a body might say, it is exaggerated from one end to the other."

" Pooh—pooh," exclaimed his worship, "your news travels with a snail's pace—I have learned any time this half hour, the doleful tidings of poor Jack Wintour's death, and by this, it is a noble to a penny that the murderer is overtaken."

" Why there it is," replied the head-borough, —" there it is—marry, there it is ! A man is taken up, as it were, and set down, too, if I may be so bold to say as much, in your worship's worshipful presence, before he can deliver himself, be he ne'er so stupendous in his brevity."

" To the point, good Master Goosecap," said the mayor, interrupting him—"to the point; for I must forth on business."

" I am an old man, now," quoth Giles, " and have grown grey and honourable in mine office, as you see; for I do well remember, it was on the very day our gracious queen was born—no I am wrong,—it was on the very day her gracious father married her gracious mother —the fair Anna Bullen,—"

" To do which," interrupted Peverell, " he, with no grace at all, put away his most virtuous and saint-like queen, the Lady Katherine."

" I remember that too," continued Giles ; " but I am a peaceable man, as a discreet constable ought to be, seeing it is his vocation to keep the peace—and therefore I never meddle with matters that don't belong to the parish— but as I was saying—Out upon it ! I am a villain if I have not clean forgot what it was I was saying.—Well, well!—to think how a man's wits may decay before his body, though they be the elder born."

"Have you clean forgot what you came about?" said his worship impatiently.

"Marry have I not, and I was coming to it. an' I had not been circumvented, by your worship and my master here.—But touching the doleful death of poor Jack Wintour"—

"I tell thee," exclaimed the mayor, with increasing impatience, "I know all about it!"

"By the mass, then," quoth Goosecap, "'tis more than I do; and yet, methinks I ought to be the first comprised, when any offence against her majesty's lieges is committed; that I may, forthwith, that is with all convenient despatch, which is as much as to say, diligently or without prevarication, pursue the offender. But let that pass. Your worship is acquainted, which is enough; you will impart to me your constructions upon the business anon:—and I have a head to contrive the best manner, when I am properly distrusted, for inventing a knave's escape. But now to the present matter.—The Abbey must be exercised, your worship—that is, it must be enchanted—or, in other words, the foul fiend must be laid by the heels, or no honest man, who is an honest man, and has the fear of Satan before his eyes, will live in St. Albans."

" Why, what's the matter now ?" said Peverell quickly.

" The matter !" quoth Giles —" by St. Nicholas, he were a better scholar than I am, who could tell you, Master Peverell. But this I know : there swims no goose in all England, an' there be not a hundred and more, of our townsmen, housewives and bairnes not reckoned, who are listening, with pale cheeks, and up-turned eyes, to the bellowing of Beelzebub."

" Be explicit, if you can," said Peverell, impatiently, and half angrily.

" I will," replied Goosecap, " I will, as thou shalt see. I was e'en at my breakfast, when—"

" Never mind your breakfast—what of the Abbey ?" interrupted his worship.

" Well then," quoth the head-borough, " I will not be implicit — but to the matter at once."

" Aye," responded Peverell, " that is what we would have."

" I know it," said Giles, " and thus it was. When I had finished my breakfast—"

" You went to the Abbey," said Peverell, anxious to get Goosecap so far, at any rate.

" No," quoth Giles, " I did not go to the Abbey—the more is the pity—for if I had, perchance—"

At this moment Crab entered, who informed his master that there were four or five of the townsfolk who craved a word with him ; and, he added, " they inquired whether Master Peverell was here."

" What is their business ?" said his worship.

" I did not ask," replied Crab, " but they told me to say they had come from the Abbey."

" Bring them hither," said his worship.
" They will tell, at once, what this dotard
would, but cannot."

" Dotard !" exclaimed Goosecap,—" dotard !
Take mine office, if I have lived too long !
Take mine office, if I have revived my powers
to reform its injunctions—if—"

The worthy head-borough was cut short in
the midst of his appeal, by the entrance of half-
a-dozen of the towns-people, who soon enabled
Peverell to understand what was the matter.
It was clear to him, from their statement, that
Overbury had been locked in over night, and
that he was then battering at the doors, and
exercising his lungs, in search of a speedy
deliverance. Peverell, therefore, briefly ex-
plained the circumstance to his worship, and
hastening to his own house for the keys, proceeded instantly to the Abbey; where he found,
as Goosecap had said, an assemblage of nearly
two hundred persons, collected by the roaring
and clatter of the enraged Overbury. They,

not being in the secret, looked at Peverell with astonishment when he approached the doors for the purpose of unlocking them. They trembled for *his* safety; but they took care of their own, by taking to their heels; expecting nothing less, when the doors were opened, than to see some fiend or goblin let loose among them. And truth to say, their fears for Peverell, as well as their own terrors, seemed likely to be realized.

Overbury looked more like a devil than a human being when he rushed forth. His face and garments were besmeared with blood; for groping about in the dark, he had upset the body of Vehan, and fallen with it into the gory stream which had flowed from his wounds. He cared little or nothing about having had such a grisly companion all night; but believing the affront had been put upon him designedly, he was incensed almost to madness. His first impulse was to aim a desperate, if not a mortal blow, with his sword at Peverell, who warded it off, though not without receiving a severe cut on his right arm. He repaid this by closing with him, dashing him to the earth, and then planting his foot upon his throat. Overbury, who was stunned by the fall, lay, for a moment, as if he were dead; while they who looked on at a distance, believing it was nothing less than a struggle between Peverell and the goblin with the iron hand, when they saw Overbury lying motionless at the feet of the former, raised a loud shout of triumph. Peverell beckoned them to approach, which they did, though cautiously; and then stooping down, to wrest the weapon out of Overbury's hand, which he still held with a firm grasp, he bade them raise him up.

"Are you mad?" he exclaimed, as Overbury opened his eyes, and stared wildly about him. "Else, why this blow?" and he pointed to his arm.

"Mad!" repeated Overbury: "no, nor fool. Hell confound you! say I, an' you dare play your scurvy tricks on me! I am no

hilding, to be flouted by you and your sleek
companions; no galliass, to be run down by a
proud carrack !—Why was I locked into yon
place last night ?—If you like me not, bid me
hence, as men should; and if I do not choose
to budge, I'll give you manly cause wherefore.
But I'll stab the tallest he among you, and
swing for it, ere you shall practise on me thus !"

Overbury who foamed with rage, while he
roared out these words, was wrought up to
such a pitch of fury, by the recollection of the
supposed insult, as well as galled by the manner in which Peverell had thrown and disarmed
him, that if he had not been held back, he
would certainly, defenceless as he was, have
sprung upon Peverell again, who listened
calmly to him, while several of his neighbours
were engaged in binding a napkin round his
wounded arm.

" You are in no condition," said he, " for ex-
postulation, or for receiving the truth of that
which happened."

" The truth !" vociferated Overbury: " What
can you tell me more than I know? You
cannot tell me I slept in my bed last night."

" But I can tell you why you did not,"
replied Peverell, in a tone of quiet scorn. " It
was because you were drunk, and asleep, before
you could get there."

The by-standers laughed at this retort,
which Overbury answered only by a look of
such collected ferocity, and appalling fierceness, that Peverell himself involuntarily shrunk
beneath the almost withering glance of this
human fiend.

" Give me my sword," said he ; " and le
me begone."

Peverell restored his weapon to him, which
he sullenly sheathed, while muttering execra-
tions that were but imperfectly heard ; and
turning upon his heel, swaggered towards his
home.

Before Peverell left the spot, he fastened the
doors of the Abbey, which he avoided entering,

on account of those who were assembled; not wishing that the body of Vehan should become either a spectacle for mere vulgar curiosity, or a topic of popular exaggeration. In his way homewards, he called upon Walwyn, whom he found in much distress of mind, though less so than on the preceding night. He delivered the keys into his custody, that he might be enabled to have the corse of his unhappy kinsman removed ; and after mentioning slightly the scene which had occurred between himself and Overbury, he hastened to his own house, where proper dressings were applied to his arm, by Peter Simcox, whom he sent for immediately.

CHAPTER II.

HELEN was leaning on her father's arm, and walking up and down the terrace, listening anxiously to his account of all the circumstances connected with the death of Vehan, when Robin came bounding along towards them.

" I have a message," said he, with an air of whimsical embarrassment.

" Deliver it, then," said Lacy.

" Aye, but it is for my lady mistress," quoth Robin.

" Then tell it me," replied Helen.

" Aye, but it is for the silent ear of your ladyship's self," added Robin, with an arch expression of countenance.

"Oh—a secret," rejoined Lacy, smiling,
" Very well—whisper it discreetly, while I say
good morrow to the swans;" and disengaging
his arm from Helen, he walked towards a
translucent piece of water, on whose surface
floated seven or eight of those birds of proud
motion and graceful beauty.

Robin now tripped up to Helen, and with a
laughing, roguish eye, half whispered in her
ear, " Fitz-Maurice !"

"What of him?" exclaimed Helen, while
her cheek grew pale.

"That is all he bade me say," replied Robin,
wondering and frightened at the agitation of
his mistress.

" Where is he?" added Helen.

" In the yellow tapestry chamber," said
Robin, sadly, as if he felt he had committed
some fault.

" Enough !" replied Helen ; " go."

Robin walked away, with a slow and dejected air.

" Has the knave forgotten himself," said

Lacy, advancing towards his daughter, and noticing the slow step, and downcast visage of poor Robin. "He looks like a rebuked offender. What is it?"

Helen acquainted her father with the communication she had received.

"Fitz-Maurice here!" he exclaimed; "let us in. He is our general; and we serve under him, sworn soldiers of mystery, for three nights to come."

Helen took her father's arm, and they returned towards the house. She was silent and trembling; for she at once dreaded, and desired, an interview with Fitz-Maurice.

When they entered the room in which he was, he advanced, took Helen by the hand, and as he led her to a seat, pressed the finger on which she wore the signet, as if to satisfy himself that it had not been removed.

"It is a noble confidence and fidelity!" he exclaimed, gently, as he bowed to Helen, and quitted her hand.

" You came not last night," said Lacy, ad-dressing Fitz-Maurice.

" But I was with you," he replied.

" With us !" repeated Lacy.

" Even as *I* say ;" continued Fitz-Maurice, " not as *you* apprehend me."

" You know, then—"

" I would know nothing, now," said Fitz-Maurice, interrupting him, " but whether I may be vouchsafed some half hour's speech with this lady."

Lacy looked at Helen : her eyes met his. They seemed to implore compliance with the request of Fitz-Maurice. He hesitated. A faint flush mantled on his cheek ; for a little of the soldier's quick and choleric spirit had been awakened by the abrupt and peremptory man-ner of Fitz-Maurice ; who, perceiving it, took his hand, and exclaimed,

" Words are but air. I could frame my en-treaty in the picked phrases of a courtier, if I did not know, an honest purpose best avouches

itself in the simplicity of its confession. I came
to confer with your daughter. Shall I return
defeated ?"

" No !" replied Lacy ; and erecting himself
into an attitude of complacent dignity, (at once
satisfied to yield, as a point of courtesy, what
he would have refused to petulant command,)
he quitted the chamber with a stately step.

" You come, as I would have you," said
Helen, after a pause. " I am grievously
afflicted with doubts and fears. You alone can
resolve the one, and—if they can be removed,
remove the other. Am I to tell you, or are
you cognizant, of all that befel me at Margery
Ashwell's ?

" Cognizant !" responded Fitz-Maurice.

" Then, speak !—The worst, whate'er of bad
must be—the best, whate'er of good can be, to
mitigate that worst. I have gone too far, to
turn back ; not far enough, to stop. I could
not live a week, oppressed by such dark fancies
as now throng about me—tormented by such

shadows of the future, as thicken round me. I
should grow desperate, and do some deed to
make my memory abhorred."

There was a marked change in the manner
of Helen. She felt, as she had ever felt, the
enthralling influence of Fitz-Maurice's presence; but she now felt, also, that come what
might, the burden which weighed her down
could be removed or lightened, only by him.
And it suited the natural energy of her character, when a difficulty presented itself, sus-
ceptible of no choice as to the means of vanquishing it, to embrace, at once, and at every
hazard, the single remedy which offered. It
was too late to consider how it had been created; it alone remained to her to determine
how it could be overcome.

" You have proved the signet's magic
power," said Fitz-Maurice.

" I have !" replied Helen ; shuddering at the
recollection of what had followed.

" But," — continued Fitz-Maurice, " you have proved it only ONCE."

" Only once !" repeated Helen.

" And *only* once," he proceeded, in the same deep, calm tone, " your startled eyes beheld the diamond words of that crystalline jewel, which Peverell carries now."

" Therein, too," replied Helen, with increasing agitation, " have I been confounded ! And in sooth, I hardly wonder more at what I have seen and heard, than at myself, a fond, weak woman, to find I keep my own counsel, and can bury all in the silent volume of my own heart."

" The million," answered Fitz-Maurice, " might so wonder, in ignorance of what thou art, and judging by the many of the few : but Helen Lacy denies herself, and dishonours Heaven's noblest work, when she thus deems of herself."

" Flattery is a bright summer garment," replied Helen, gravely, " that should be worn with the gawds of fortune: it is too thin and garish, for the dark winter of my condition. Unfold, I pray you, the index of this strange book, on whose mystic leaves is inscribed my sad destiny. I have that within me, which will let me read it."

" You *have* read it !" said Fitz-Maurice. " It was contained in those four glittering lines !—It lies in those two behests."

" What behests ?" asked Helen.

" The signet !—" replied Fitz-Maurice, and he paused.

" I understand," added Helen, thoughtfully. " Further trials await me ! I must re-visit that scene of horror—I must again gaze, with an aching sight and almost frenzied brain, upon those midnight spells—again I must drag from that vexed and tortured spirit, Alascon, what the mightiest of earth's sons could not buy with all their thrones and sovereignties, wanting the further price which I paid down ! Oh ! this is terrible."

" This would be terrible," said Fitz-Maurice,
" if this were so ; but it is not."

" How !" exclaimed Helen ; " it is not so ?"

" No, gentle maiden ! But now hear me.—
That which remains undone—THOU only canst
do. For, as the blade which smokes with
bloody execution in the shock of battle, would
shiver in the hand that wields it, were it not
duly tempered ; so thou, called to the issue of
this great mystery, would faint beneath it,
hadst thou not passed through the furnace of
that fierce ordeal. It was thy appointed preparation ; the test, though you knew it not,
by which your fitness to perform the crowning
act, was tried ; and he who can slay a giant,
must, perforce, have sinews to wrestle with a
dwarf. The holy love that kindled in your
heart its strong desire to know the future—the
undaunted spirit which fed that desire—and the
heroic fortitude which accomplished it, proclaimed the matchless being, whose ripe qualities for the achievement of a long fore-told

triumph, I have sought through many a land.
You have said truly. You cannot go back.
You cannot stop. What then remains? To
advance. But whither, and how far? Two
steps !—The first, to aid – the second, to
possess—a symbol of inestimable value ! I see
amazement staring in your eyes. I read there,
the conflict of your soul. I read an earnest
supplication, too, for words, which I may not
utter. No, Helen Lacy ! Not even that eloquent, though mute prayer—nor, if that angel
look were followed by all the witchery of woman's tongue, sanctified, as here it would be,
by all the holiest of woman's virtues, could I,
DARE I, breathe, what your distracted heart
pants to hear ! For this is now your only trial.
It is now only demanded of you, (to fulfil what
is begun,) that you have SILENT FAITH, and an
unshaken, an unassailable resolution. Believe
that what you are to do, is good ; and then,
shrink not from the doing. Remember the
portentous replications of Alascon ;—remember

the mighty triumph, or the unutterable misery, that is suspended on *your* will ;—remember of whom it was prophesied, that he should win the triumph,—Even he, who won you! I conjure you, then—"

" Stop !" exclaimed Helen, in a voice convulsed with agitation—" or bid me remember, also, the horrid condition that was attached.— Blood!—more blood must be shed!—ay, and shed by the hand to which it is most precious! Bid me remember, too, those frightful visions of the mystic glass, when I grew frantic, and dashed myself to earth, that I might see no more! What is it you would have me do, thou man of mystery?—The vulture grew to likeness of myself !—Am I to play the human vulture? To drink the life-blood of my father,—even at its sacred font ?—That heart which has been my sanctuary; which has never known a feeling towards me that was not gentle, kind, and loving? God! God! deliver me, in thy mercy, from this sharp trial, or mine own heart will surely break !"

Helen wept in agony. Fitz-Maurice gazed upon her in silence; but with a troubled spirit. When her grief abated, he spoke.

" Why this sorrow ?" said he. " What though your hand were on a cup, drugged with deadliest poison ? Still, if there were no power to make you drain it, you might look upon the mortal draught with an undisturbed brow. So reason this matter. You apprehend a deed of horror. But there is no malignant planet which over-rules your will. Say you cannot banish these sick fancies of your brain—that this dream of a heated imagination pursues you ? The worst that can befal thee, is to groan a little longer under its harrowing influence : for you are as free, as the eagle in his mountain home, who cleaves the air above their highest tops, the monarch of illimitable space ! But *can* you rest upon the wing ? Having taken your daring

flight, *can* you hover, beneath the clouds,
through which you must pass to find a resting
place, and watch till they disperse? For so
you must do, if here you pause. And forget
not, that though *you* pause, others do not ; that
whatever is to be, will be; and that all the consolation which may await you, will be to know,
not that you *have* arrested, in its course, the dark
tide of human misery,—but that you *might !*"

" Spare me !" ejaculated Helen. " I am
tottering on the brink of a dismal abyss, dark-
ling and alone ; and need thy friendly hand to
guide me from it; not thy deluding voice to
beguile me onward !"

Fitz-Maurice rose, and approaching Helen,
leaned in a careless but graceful attitude against
the chair in which she was seated. Her heart
beat quicker, and her bosom heaved with unde-
fined emotions at this sudden and unexpected
movement of Fitz-Maurice ; but she did not
withdraw her face from the handkerchief, bathed
with her tears, in which she had buried it.

" If,"—said he, in a deep, thrilling tone; " if
there were in this world, a being who, for more
years than he was permitted to tell, had languished in captivity—if his chains were forged
by no human hand, rivetted by no human
power—if his dungeon walls were nor of stone,
nor of brass, nor ribbed with iron—if his doom
were such, that no natural tear could ever
gather in his sleep-forbidden eyes—no bursting
sigh, could ever discharge the grief that clung
to his long-withering heart — if, for him, the
seasons had no change, and time itself stood
still—if the fresh spring gladdened not *his*
cheek—the warm and glorious sun of summer,
glowed not in *his* veins—the temperate autumn,
with its delicious western gale, fanned not *his*
brow—nor icy winter drove *him* to the festal
board, and social hearth—if there were one so
lone, so blighted, on this fair earth, who, kneeling at your feet, should say, in trembling hope,
and suppliant agony, strike off my fetters, for
thou can'st—throw wide my prison doors, for

thou hast the key in thy hands—could you spurn him from you?"

Helen raised her eyes. Fitz-Maurice had fallen on one knee; and she saw him in the very attitude, and with the same imploring look, that she had beheld in the charmed mirror of Alascon! Before she could speak, or hardly recal her bewildered thoughts, the door burst open, and Mephosto stood before them. Helen gazed with terror upon his hideous aspect and menacing look.

" Rise !" he exclaimed.

" The hour ?" said Fitz-Maurice.

" The sun is hot upon my cheek !" answered Mephosto.

" Slave, thou liest !" replied Fitz-Maurice. " This is thy malignant spite."

" Ha !" said the dwarfish fiend, " then is thy doom come! I bid thee once! Hark! thy charger neighs in answer;" and he crawled nearer to Fitz-Maurice.

" There must be time for the scritch owl to

c 2

cry thrice ere thou bid me again," answered
Fitz-Maurice. Then turning to Helen, with a
wild and frantic look, he added, " Oh, lady !
Fail me now, and fail me ever !"

" Rise! I bid you twice !" croaked forth
Mephosto, as he dragged himself closer to the
still kneeling Fitz-Maurice, while he drew his
jewel-hilted dagger, and looked at Helen with
a terrific glance. " Hark ! your courser churns
the bit with a foaming mouth !"

" He must to his crib, i' the centre of the
earth, and back again, and bring thy dagger's
point envenomed, ere thou bid me thrice !" exclaimed Fitz-Maurice, with a suffocated voice.
Then, once more turning to Helen, he seized
her hand, pointed to the signet, and in accents
hardly articulate, " Command him, as thou
didst Alascon," said he, " or see me perish !"

Helen scarcely understood him ; but she saw
the blade of Mephosto's dagger kindle at the
point into what appeared a flame of blood.
He had raised it aloft—his eyes flashed fire—

the chamber shook beneath him—and his hand was upon Fitz-Maurice, whose face grew livid and convulsed.

" Rise !" roared Mephosto in a voice of thunder. " I have called you ONCE—I have called you TWICE—I call you—

Helen tore off her glove, and stretching forth her hand, exclaimed, with a kind of hysterical laugh, " I COMMAND thee, OBEY THE SIGNET !"

A loud yell followed from Mephosto. He crawled away. In a moment after, the clattering of horses' feet was heard without, and Fitz-Maurice, springing up, caught Helen in his arms, as she swooned from the excessive agitation of her feelings.

Helen soon recovered, and when she opened her eyes, she saw Fitz-Maurice standing by her side, contemplating her with a look full of deep devotion, while, at the same time, his features were lighted up with an intense expression of conscious satisfaction. She could plainly read what were his emotions that mo-

ment : fervent gratitude, and new born hope !
His hair, which clustered in profusion over his
forehead, had slightly parted, and she beheld,
for the first time, the crimson wound which
marked his brow. Its colour seemed to come
and go, changing each instant from a pale to a
vivid red, as if it followed the throbbing motion of his blood. Fitz-Maurice observed the
direction of her eyes, and gently drew his hair
together, so as to cover his forehead.

" What am I to understand," said Helen,
" from that which I have witnessed ?   What,
from that which I have heard ?   Can you not
now unfold the sequel ?   It would seem," she
continued, looking at the signet, " that almost
without knowing how, I have performed one
of those two behests you spoke of. What is
the other—and what will it achieve ?   Alas ! I
sought the fatal knowledge I possess, to save
a father—must I employ it only to—"

" Save the tears of future orphans ? to
stay the havock which blood cannot satiate ?

to purchase eternal life among the holiest of the saints of heaven? and to snatch, from the dominion of hell, a symbol of righteousness?" interrupted Fitz-Maurice.

"If these things could be," replied Helen, "and if so unworthy, so weak and so frail a creature as myself, could be their instrument, yet surely it would be appointed I should work by more hallowed means. What, if I am in the toils of the arch-fiend, and blindly executing his will, to the everlasting perdition of my most precious soul? Oh! one thought of that would mad me quite!"

"I repeat," said Fitz-Maurice, "that you must have silent faith, and an unshaken resolution, to fulfil what you have begun."

"On what must that faith rest?" answered Helen.

"On this!" exclaimed Fitz-Maurice, with an awful solemnity of manner, drawing aside his hair, and pointing to the burning cross which seemed, at that moment, to glow like living fire upon his brow.

"Mysterious being!" said Helen, "What art thou?"

"Mortal, like thyself!" he answered. "An undaunted soldier of Christ; one who hath kissed the true sepulchre—and been ordained its knight, in the name of the Father, the Son, and the Holy Ghost; but whose wondrous and accursed destiny, since, for years he may not number, hath withered all human sympathies and affections within him, till now, he stands before thee, a blasted form of what he was! More than this I am forbidden to tell : nor could my tongue have uttered what it hath, hadst thou not commanded hence, by that signet's mighty potency, (whereat thou well may'st marvel,) the abhorred thing which called me. That act struck off one galling link of the chain that holds me to my fate : a fate, hopeless and irrevocable, till I shall have found what all my reviving hopes tell me, exists in

THEE! I have long pursued, but never came
so near, as now, the performance of the hard
and ruthless conditions, which must re-
store me to myself. Oh, lady! Gentle pity,
and soft compassion, build their throne of
tears and sighs, in woman's yielding heart.
She is Mercy's handmaid; and through her
lips breathe peace and consolation to the
bruised spirits of this world. One deed of
heavenly goodness more; one closing trial of
your faith—one last display of dauntless courage—and a wretch—a very wretch, whose
single hour of anguish might out-number the
groans of a mortal life of suffering, would
kiss the dust beneath your feet. Yes! Helen
Lacy! THOU ART THE WOMAN! By that age
of torment I have endured, which language
cannot shadow forth—by that present agony
which tears my soul—by that tremendous future which lies howling before me—by this
burning witness of the truth, which now
scalds my brain,—by all that man can urge, or

God, inspire, I adjure thee, be faithful to the last, and redeem me from my captivity!"

"How?" said Helen, while she gazed upon him with awe and terror, for his voice and figure, and manner, seemed more than mortal.

"How!" exclaimed Fitz-Maurice; "By the signet's power."

"Where and when?" added Helen.

"The Abbey—to-morrow night!" replied Fitz-Maurice.

"The Abbey!"

"Aye, the Abbey!" continued Fitz-Maurice. "Why comes that cloud across thy brow? Hear me. If when the chimes go twelve to-morrow night, thou, attired like a bride, in virgin white, veiled, and with that ring upon thy wedding finger, strike thrice upon the Abbey door, and at each stroke exclaim, 'Husband come, the cross is mine,' the portal straight shall open. Then enter. Speak not, whate'er thou seest. But, advancing to the altar, stand beneath it, and casting back thy veil, take off the signet. Place it on the altar, kneel, and pray in these words, ' *Forgive me : I know not what I do, but thy will be mine.*' Then rise ; place the signet again upon thy finger, and raising it to Heaven exclaim, ' *I com. mand thee, obey !*' What is to follow, it were the forfeiture of all to tell ; but mark, this must you do in silent faith—no ear must hear, no heart must know, thy intents. And if this you can do—if this you will do,—if no terror of what you behold, appal you,—if no dread beset you, when prayers, and threats, and imprecations assail you, the triumph is complete !''

Fitz-Maurice paused. Helen sat pale and trembling. In imagination, she was already performing the frightful task assigned her, when suddenly she started up, and shrieking aloud, exclaimed—" But my father,—oh, God ! My father ! what of him ?"

" Is it a vision that troubles you ?" said Fitz-Maurice.

" No, no," replied Helen, weeping. " Me-

mory, too faithful to its office, brings before
my fancy the wizard mirror of Alascon. Blood
that is precious to the hand which sheds it,
must flow ere this triumph is achieved ; and
what blood on earth so precious as that which
I have endured all this to spare ?"

"Then you deny me !" said Fitz-Maurice.

"I do not," answered Helen ; "but I am
almost mad.   Husband ! what husband ?—He
is my husband, lover, father, all ! Whom do I
demand, when I bid my husband come? Away
—you mock me to undo me !"

"Then   you   deny   me !" repeated   Fitz-
Maurice.

"*My* bridal dress, alas ! should be my winding sheet ; *my* bridal bed, my coffin ; death,
grim, bony death, my husband ! Oh ! how I
could wind my arms round his rattling bones,
and sink to rest upon my pillow of worms !"

"Then you deny me !" still repeated Fitz-
Maurice, but in a tone of voice unlike any

which Helen had heard from him. She looked at him. He fixed his eyes wildly upon her.

"Can I be satisfied," said she, "that the living grave I dig thee from, shall not be my father's sepulchre?"

The door opened, and Mephosto entered again. He spoke not; but with his hand silently beckoned Fitz-Maurice to follow.

"I come!" said he.

Helen threw herself into a chair and wept aloud.

Mephosto beckoned.

"I come!" repeated Fitz-Maurice. He seized the hand of Helen; she raised her eyes towards him, swimming in tears. "Peerless maiden!" he exclaimed,—"Bride of Christ!—dost thou deny me? Speak! For my fate calls me hence."

Mephosto beckoned once more, and stamped violently on the ground.

"Say no!" exclaimed Fitz-Maurice, "or I am lost."

A loud laugh burst from Mephosto.

" No !" cried Helen faintly, and sunk back in her chair.

" Angel of life !" ejaculated Fitz-Maurice, and hurried out of the room. Helen, though hardly conscious of any thing, heard the departing tramp of his courser's feet, and only felt that a terrible scene was over.

In a few minutes she rallied her distracted thoughts sufficiently to hasten to her own chamber. She was most anxious to do so, lest her father, knowing she was alone, should seek an interview with her, which she was utterly incapable of sustaining.

CHAPTER III.

At seven o'clock, De Clare, Mortimer, Peverell, and the rest, met at Lacy's. Overbury
was among them, having learned from Hungerford Hoskyns the hour that had been appointed.
His look and manner indicated that the circumstance of the preceding night still rankled in
his mind ; but as it was known only to Peverell
and Walwyn that he had actually been locked
in, the others were at a loss to account for his
more than ordinary fierce, yet sullen deportment. There had been no time for explanation,
when De Clare, addressing Peverell, inquired

what accident had befallen him, seeing he carried his arm in a sling. The latter not caring
to revive the occurrence of the morning, by de-
scribing how he had received his wound, answered carelessly that it was a mere trifle which '
he would take another opportunity of mentioning.

The conversation then turned upon the murder of mine host, the news of which had, of
course, spread rapidly throughout the town ;
when De Clare informed them that he had
called upon his worship, not half an hour since,
and no tidings had then been received of the
assassin. The event was considered by all of
them, as no less extraordinary than lamentable,
on account of the apparent absence of all the
usual incentives to such a deed. Neither
plunder, nor revenge, seemed to have instigated
the murderer ; and why, therefore, he had
committed the crime at all, was pronounced
wholly inexplicable.

" But that is not the only inexplicable part

of the business," observed Peverell; "for I
learn that the body of his father, which was
placed in the charnel house, has been removed.
The coffin was found empty, this afternoon,
when the persons went thither to convey it to the
church-yard for interment. I can easily believe,
however, that his son removed it, before he
fled; for the door was not locked."

"But to what purpose?" said Lacy.

"That I cannot tell," replied Peverell.—
"But when I recal his extraordinary history of
himself, and the terrific picture he drew of
those three days and nights, during which he
sat by his wretched father to see him die, I can
conceive many motives calculated to influence
such a being, which I should discard in my estimate of any other man's reasons for whatever
he might do. It is likely enough, that in the
wild suggestions of his mind, he either dug a
road-side grave for his father's bones; or has
borne them, perhaps, to some dark and obscure
spot, there to lie beside them, and await the

slow death of famine himself. Either of these methods of disposing of the miserably-wasted remains, would be quite consistent with his moody character. Depend upon it, he will not be taken alive; for if it had been his intention to be so found, he would have been. Whatever cause he had to destroy that poor man, (and there appears no reasonable ground to doubt the fact of his being the murderer), he would have abided voluntarily his own justification of it, if he had not resolved, before-hand, upon the means to defy justice. It is my firm opinion, I confess, either that he will never be discovered, or, that at some future day, his bones will be found whitening by the side of his father's, in some pathless glen or solitary cave."

"I think you are right;" said De Clare, "but we shall miss mine host to-night. His jovial face, and ever merry eye, which still laughed in spite of his sometimes quaking heart, were the best antidotes to melancholy I e'er looked upon."

"By my faith," exclaimed Mortimer, "talking of poor Jack Wintour, quickens my dull memory. Friend Overbury, where did you sleep last night?"

"Where you did not;" replied Overbury, sullenly, "and where, had you, you would have given your trim mustachios to be away."

"You say truly;" retorted Mortimer, "for to sleep where you did, I must have had you for a bed-fellow, and I would have offered my head as well as my mustachios to be excused so unsavory a companion. But impart: how was it? We despatched our departed host of *The Rose* to look for you, and you were gone."

"Indeed we did, mark you;" added Owen Rees, "and he vociferated three times; but you answered not, mark you, as one gentleman should when another calls him."

"He burns in hell, for that lie!" exclaimed Overbury, "an' he said so."

"It was no lie, Mister Overbury, mark you," replied Owen, "if you did not answer; and if you were not in the Abbey—as Heaven forbid you were, for it was a lack-comfort bed—why then, mark you, how could you answer, Mister Overbury?"

"What is it you mean?" said Overbury, furiously. "Am I here to be baited? If so, let me see the man among you, who will step forth and begin the sport! Hell's torments be my portion, if I do not cleave to the chine, the gibing fool that does it, though all your swords were hilted in me the next moment! The fire of hell blister your glib tongues, an' their frothy quips gird at me! Is it not enough that your baboon's tricks have prospered? I have faced danger on the salt sea, and looked to find my grave a hundred fathom beneath its foam, too long, to be frighted now by the cawing of such choughs."

Peverell here interposed, and related what had taken place between himself and Over-bury; observing, in conclusion, that his crip-

pled arm bore testimony to the angry feelings
which the accident had provoked.

"Accident!" muttered Overbury. "Such
accidents happen always, when men play the
boy, and blubber for the mischief they dare
not confess as such."

"Thou art tongue-valiant," said Mortimer,
stepping close to Overbury, with his hand upon
his sword, "but nothing more with honest
men. I tell thee, to thy teeth, that thou wert
drunk last night; that, in thy drunkenness,
thou sleptst; that, in thy sleep, we missed
thee; that, missing thee, we sought thee; that,
seeking thee, we did thee a kinder office than
thy brutish quality deserved; and now, deny
this to my teeth, if thou darst, thou sea-mon-
ster!"

"And when thou hast done so," added the
little Welshman, strutting fiercely up to Overbury, "call me mountain goat, again—Wilfrid
Overbury, some time master of *the Scorpion!*"

Overbury's cheek turned pale, at the mention of *the Scorpion*, and he looked at Owen Rees as if he would read in his face, whether he had a meaning beyond the more repetition of words that had been used by Fitz-Maurice.

" I do not deny the drink," said he ; " but it was an ungracious trick to leave me with that bloody man in that dark, cold place.   I rolled upon him, and we fell ; and thinking it was—I know not what—I stabbed him thrice as he lay beneath me, ere I remembered what had happened.   It was an ungracious trick, I say, to leave me thus."

Walwyn was much affected by this declaration of Overbury, and uttered some half-stifled exclamation of distress.   Every one present, indeed, felt shocked, no less at the churlish apathy with which he described the horrid indignity offered to the body of Vehan, than at the idea of the hideous scuffle, which their imaginations at once pictured, with such a ruffian as Overbury ; who fancied he was butchering an opponent, instead of striking at a corse.

A pause of several minutes ensued, which De Clare at length interrupted, by inquiring at what hour they should proceed to the Abbey, and whether they were to see Fitz-Maurice that night. Peverell proposed nine o'clock; but with regard to Fitz-Maurice, he could say nothing, for he had not seen him since he was last present among them all. Lacy mentioned that he had been with him that day.

" Again *here !*" exclaimed Peverell. " And what said he ?"

" To me, nothing," replied Lacy, " for he came to have an interview with my daughter; and what passed, I have not heard."

" An interview with your daughter," said Peverell, musing.

" He'll woo her, by my faith !" observed Mortimer.

" As the lion would woo the hind," replied

De Clare, " or the eagle the dove! His character, truly, is formed to win woman's love;
but it will be, when the wolf and the lamb
browse the same herbage, or summer roses blow
at Christmas."

" He is no amorous gallant, certainly," said
Lacy; " but this is the second time he has
visited Helen."

" Look to it!" responded Mortimer : " look
to it, my friend! I do not say your daughter
will fall from her duty; but I do say that a
woman will sometimes fall, like snow in June,
most strangely, and when men expect it
not."

" If your experience has taught you so
much," replied De Clare, " I am converted;
but, inasmuch as you are yet a bachelor, I hold
to my opinion."

" Which is——" said Mortimer.

" That women have eyes," answered De
Clare, " and do not choose husbands, as the
mole works—without them."

" Your experience," retorted Mortimer,
" has taught you so much ; and there be more
in this good company, or I am at fault, who
could supply you with as good proof of your
theory as myself. But to matters of more grave
import. Might it not be well to inquire of the
Lady Helen, whether Fitz-Maurice expressed
his intention, or otherwise, of being with
us ?"

This suggestion was immediately acted upon
by Lacy, who despatched a servant to Helen ;
but the answer returned by her was, that Fitz-
Maurice had not intimated any thing on the
subject.

- " Then he will not come," said De Clare ;
" which surprises me, considering his absence
last night."

" He told me," replied Lacy, " and it was
all he did tell me, that he *was* with us last
night."

" With us !" exclaimed Peverell.

" That was my very question," continued

Lacy, " and his answer was—'even as *I* say—
not as *you* apprehend.' "

" I protest," observed Mortimer, " I wish
I could make out this two-legged riddle—this
living mystery—this Fitz-Maurice, as he calls
himself."

" His stream runs too deep for thy line," said
De Clare.

" Or for any of our lines, I think," added
Lacy. " He is like a well defended fortress,
unapproachable either by sudden attack, or
secret mining."

" Why do you waste your breath so idly ?"
exclaimed Overbury. " You have all bound
yourselves to him for three more nights of
servitude, and be he man or be he devil, you
are so long his. I am free, it is true; but it is
my humour, now, to see the end. Besides, I
have a matter to settle with him ere we part for
aye."

The intrusion of Overbury's sentiments put
an end to the conversation on this subject, for

every one abstained from replying to him ; and during the rest of the time, their discourse was chiefly with Walwyn, whose dejection was extreme. He had not once opened his lips, but sat in gloomy silence, brooding over the sad fate which had befallen his kinsman. The circumstance mentioned by Overbury had added much to the poignancy of his feelings.

They endeavoured to withdraw him from his melancholy reflections : but it was evident the blow had fallen heavily upon him. In spite of every remonstrance, of every argument, or persuasion, he accused himself as the rash murderer of Vehan, whose memory he now seemed to idolize with that passionate grief which magnifies what it mourns by its own estimate, rather than by the value reason assigns. It is one advantage, however, of such grief, that if its pangs be sharp, they are brief : for as the sorrow wears away, its estimate diminishes; while the more severe privation, over which our reason mourns, endures till the mind itself decays.

In the midst of this various conversation, the time arrived for proceeding to the Abbey, and they quitted Lacy's house. But they had scarcely reached the place, when they were surprised by the sound of horses' feet rapidly approaching; and before the doors were unlocked, Fitz-Maurice, followed by Mephosto, halted in the midst of them. Fitz-Maurice, as usual, instantly alighted, and the next moment, Mephosto was off at the same furious rate.

"We knew not of your coming," said De Clare, "and had ceased to expect you."

"I knew of yours," replied Fitz-Maurice, "and came. I have business to do to-night."

They entered the Abbey, and, advancing to the table, took their seats. Fitz-Maurice occupied the same place as on the first night. Peverell and Lacy were on each side of him; De Clare at the opposite end of the table; and the rest were ranged all on one side. Overbury, therefore, sat entirely alone. His deportment was less boisterous than on the preceding night; but he had no sooner seated himself, than he filled out a cup of wine, which he immediately drank off.

CHAPTER IV.

PEVERELL related to Fitz-Maurice the tragical incident of Vehan's death, with all the circumstances which preceded and accompanied it. Fitz-Maurice listened with seeming attention; but there was an evident expression of gladness in his eye, as he turned it upon Walwyn, when Peverell mentioned how deep was his affliction for the untoward event.

" He was his friend?" said Fitz-Maurice.

" He was more," replied Peverell, " for he was his well-beloved kinsman too."

Fitz-Maurice made no answer; and Peverell

went on to state the extraordinary occurrence of
Wintour's murder, prefacing it with a brief
account of the singular history of the Venetian
youth, his supposed murderer. Fitz-Maurice
appeared less attentive to this than he had been
to what concerned Vehan; and when Peverell
ceased, it was manifest that he had sunk into a
profound abstraction.

The presence of Fitz-Maurice, his mysterious
air, his silence, and the restless glances which he
ever and anon cast round the Abbey, tended, in
conjunction with their own recollection of past,
and their anticipation of future events, to diffuse
a more than ordinary gloom. Overbury was the
only one who seemed insensible to this feeling.
He. did not speak; but he drained cup after
cup of wine, as if he were drinking himself up
to some required pitch of excitement. Occa-
sionally he directed his looks towards Fitz-
Maurice; but if, by chance, their eyes met, he
withdrew his with marked perturbation; his
cheeks became flushed, and he eagerly sought

to hide his confusion, by renewing his potations.

They had remained thus for nearly an hour, when a thundering knock was heard at the door, which resounded in doubling echoes through the lofty aisles. They all started round, and Overbury sprung upon his feet. Fitz-Maurice was motionless. Before any one could speak, the knock was repeated, but much louder. They all rose, except Fitz-Maurice, who betrayed, neither by look nor gesture, the slightest participation in their amazement. A third time the knock was heard, and the solid foundations of the Abbey shook beneath their feet. Every eye was turned towards Fitz-Maurice, who still sat motionless and silent.

" What may this mean?" exclaimed De Clare.

The doors opened, and Mephosto entered. They could not at first distinguish him, through the deep gloom of the further extremity ; but they heard the patting of his broad feet along the stone pavement. At length his form became visible, as he moved to where Fitz-Maurice was seated. When he was within a yard or two of him, he fell upon his face and grovelled along the ground like a whipped spaniel.

" Am I obeyed ?" said Fitz-Maurice.

" It is done," replied Mephosto.

" Enough," answered Fitz-Maurice. " Be watchful as the lynx. Hence !"

The dwarf retired, for some paces, in the same prostrate attitude, and then raising himself upon his feet, he crawled slowly out of the Abbey.

They beheld this scene with dumb surprise ; and when they heard the doors close, resumed their seats in silence.

" It has not been always thus," said Fitz-Maurice, addressing Lacy ; " and would not be so now, but for thee and thine."

" I do not understand you," replied Lacy.

" When the grey dawn first streaks the

eastern clouds," answered Fitz-Maurice, " the
benighted traveller rejoices, but he sees not the
landscape that lies before him. By impercep-
tible degrees, its fresh and dewy loveliness grows
into form and beauty ; anon, the gorgeous sun,
in rising glory, flings his golden beams upon
the earth, and hill and valley, the woodland and
the verdant plain, the deep river and the gush-
ing mountain stream, are all revealed. Then
steps he cheerily onward, and straight forgets
the o'erpast perils of the dark night. Even so,
I say, hath it been with each of ye. But your
dawn is at hand ; your hour of sun-rise approaches, when you shall no longer ask, whither
is it we go ?"

" There is not, I believe, a flinching spirit
among us," said De Clare; " for when last we
renewed our compact with you, it was with the
resolved hearts of men self-devoted to the
worst."

" But still with such distrust of one another," added Overbury, " that, like a band of

rogues, engaged to rob or murder, you must be sworn, to hang together. Now I—"

" Prefer to hang alone," added Mortimer; " and I protest I not only commend thy choice, but languish for the performance of it."

" And when I do," vociferated Overbury, " it will be in a fit of the spleen, to think that thou canst be hanged only once, an' the rope break not."

" Which it will not do, when thou art hanged, my master of the Scorpion," retorted Mortimer; " for the devil will have the twisting of thy rope; and 'tis his pride to have his own children well hung."

" Why, there again you would mock me," exclaimed Overbury, valiant with wine. " *Master of the Scorpion!* What can you say or—"

" I," interrupted Fitz-Maurice, fixing his eyes upon him; " but that your vessel, on your homeward voyage, struck upon the Goodwin Sands, and *all* the crew perished. The ship went down. You buffetted the waves, a golden treasure girded round your waist, and gained the beach. A good old man, with warm and generous cordials, brought you back to life, led you to his lonely habitation, gave you shelter, food, and clothing; which you requited from the store you had saved, and left him."

" I did," said Overbury, " and he was thankful."

" As thou wast," added Fitz-Maurice, " when you found that YOU ALONE were saved !"

" I—I,—grieved—bitterly," stammered forth Overbury, utterly confounded by what he had heard.

" Peace !" exclaimed Fitz-Maurice, in a tone of stern command. " I promised you, erewhile, further satisfaction. You shall have it. Behold !"

Overbury sat like one spell-bound. Except that his eyes moved, and his broad chest heaved with a quick and labouring respiration, he seemed a statue, so fixed was his attitude, so bloodless his cheeks, so marble his look. There was a visible consternation, too, on the countenances of all, save Fitz-Maurice, whose features underwent not the slightest change.

While thus wrapped in suspense as to what would ensue, Fitz-Maurice took from his neck a gold chain, to which was appended a Jerusalem cross, and kissing it thrice, he exclaimed each time, "Appear!"

At the third command they heard a noise like that of a swift stream, running over a loose pebbly bed; and then they saw a steaming vapour slowly ascend from the ground, which, as it grew in bulk, spread from wall to wall, filling the whole space of the Abbey, except where they sat. It gradually assumed the appearance of the green ocean; the waves gently undulated; and upon their scarcely rippled surface fell a soft pale light, like the moonbeams. Presently, the perfect image of a ship, becalmed, its sails idly flapping in the wind as it died away, swelled into shape.

"Now pause: and, anon, follow my words," exclaimed Fitz-Maurice.

The wondrous scene remained. It was so marvellously the counterpart of reality, that they almost fancied they felt the freshness of the ocean breeze play upon their cheeks.

"Such was the night, its serene beauty such," said Fitz-Maurice, "when, some six years since, a vessel like the one you see, lay becalmed on the silver-seeming waves that wash Sicilia's shore. How unlike the peaceful scene without, was the foul act of lust and blood that passed within! A man, whose past deeds were written in the blackest page of human crime—whose already perjured soul was stained with guilt beyond the wrath of Heaven to forgive; who had rifled the poor—slain the innocent—beggared the friend who trusted him—plundered the rich—violated the sanctuary—and cut the throat of the priest on his own altar—plucked buried jewels from the dead, and ripped the matron's womb in bloody scoff, to teach a pirate's midwifery,—this man, so steeped in villainy as I have charactered him, was MASTER of the ship. As if he had meditated solely how he might do a deed, to outdo the dark catalogue of those he had committed, his devilish spirit engendered one, so monstrous, that in all hell there groans no soul doomed to its penal fires for such another! E'en as a noble sire may see himself dishonoured in his sons, so, a degenerate one shall give goodly fruit, which smacks not of the rank soil that produced it. Look at that form of innocence and beauty, and wonder, as ye may, how from a source so foul and loathsome, a creature thus rare and perfect could have sprung. She was his daughter."

At this moment, the bright shadow of a female started into life as it were, upon the deck of the phantom vessel. She appeared in the act of offering up her evening orisons, and her parted lips seemed to move, while a saint-like expression dwelt upon her young, but pensive features. Her limbs were moulded in the finest proportions, and an air of graceful modesty clothed her with bewitching loveliness. A

loud groan burst from Overbury as this vision
gradually melted away.

" The fair GONDOLINE," continued Fitz-
Maurice, " perished that night ! The ravening
monster of the deep stole upon her slumbers,
and the shrieking virgin found herself in the
hot grasp of a ravisher. Wild prayers and
screaming curses fall from her lips—supplicating
tears gush from her eyes—with frenzied strength
she struggles—with piteous accents she im-
plores—and then, in choking agony, calls upon
her father ! Happy had she died that moment
in blessed ignorance !   Alas ! she lived to know
the caitiff. IT WAS HER FATHER ! Yes,—the
spoiler was betrayed, though shrouded in darkness.   Despair and horror seized him ; and he
who shrunk not from the damned commission of
his unhallowed crime, now stood aghast at the
thought of one withering glance from the maniac eyes of his violated daughter. She was
mad !—her delirious screams of father ! father !
seared his brain, and rang his soul's knell of

everlasting perdition! This demon-lecher, who could have lived and smiled again, self-pardoned in his own pernicious heart, if his own heart were all that quailed him, could *not* live to brave an outraged world. What, then? Did he smite himself, and so appease the justice of this world, and invoke eternal judgment in the next? Behold, how for a time, his recreant nature absolved itself from both."

When Fitz-Maurice uttered these words, the phantasm upon which they gazed underwent a horrible change. What had, hitherto, appeared the calm green wave of the ocean, now heaved and rolled, a sea of blood : and on its troubled surface seemed to lie the form of GONDOLINE, ghastly and distorted—her flowing auburn hair dishevelled; her garments rent—and her fair bosom gashed with deep wounds, which looked as though they still bled. The scene grew dark—the vessel blackened in the gloom—and a dismal cry swept along the waters, as the figure of GONDOLINE

slowly sunk beneath them, deepening in its
descent, their crimson hue.   The next mo·
ment, the darkness gradually disappeared; the
waves rippled, as if a rising breeze began to
curl their foaming tops; they broke, in danc-
ing surges, against the side of the ship, whose
lately pendent sails now filled with the wind;
the brightness of the sun, succeeded to what
had been the likeness of the soft, pale moon-
light; and the tossing waves played in his
beams, like a floor of sparkling emeralds.
The ship moved.   It wore round.   And as its
stern seemed to heave in sight, " THE SCOR-
PION, WILFRID OVER'BURY, MASTER," appeared, painted in large white letters upon
a black ground !

Overbury had hitherto sat silent—gazing,
like the rest, upon the necromantic illusion;
but unlike the rest, a prey to tortures, which
no language may describe.   His swart and disfigured face was bathed with perspiration, which
ran from him in streams: his teeth gnashed:

his eyes were starting from their sockets: his breathing was short and convulsive; and as the varying torments of his awakened conscience started into visible existence upon his agitated frame and features,—now shrinking within himself—now grinning, as if in more than human scorn of that abhorrence which he felt was kindling round him—then grasping the table with a sort of frantic clutching of his half clenched hands—he exhibited an appalling image of a guilty wretch, whose long life of dark and desperate crime, was suddenly unveiled, and placed in terrible array before him.

When, however, the vision had thus awfully pronounced " THOU ART THE MAN !" he could no longer command his maddened feelings, but, starting up and drawing his sword, he rushed towards Fitz-Maurice like a chafed tiger, roaring out " Fiend! devil !—have at thy throat, hell-dog, an' thou canst be strangled !"

He staggered—reeled—fell—rolled for a

moment on the ground in contortions of the most violent agony—raised himself on his knees —gazed wildly round—saw the spectre of his murdered daughter, rising from the bosom of the once more becalmed sea, apparelled in glory, like an angel, and ascending to the clouds : then, with horrid imprecations, which burst from him in loud yells, rather than in human accents, fell back and lay motionless.

At that moment, the scene of enchantment vanished ! Howling and laughing were heard without ; the doors flew open ; Mephosto entered—he crawled towards the body of Overbury, seized it by the throat, and with the same ease that he would have thrown his mantle round him, flung it over his shoulder, and carried it out of the Abbey.

CHAPTER V.

DURING the whole of these marvellous and mysterious proceedings, Fitz-Maurice maintained a dignified self-possession. Not the slightest perturbation was perceptible, even when the infuriate Overbury sprung from his seat, and rushed towards him. He looked at him, as a superior being might be supposed to do; conscious that he was invulnerable, or secure in his certain knowledge of what was to happen. The rest, though agitated by a variety of emotions, were but mute spectators of all that passed.

" This at least, is no mystery," said Fitz-
Maurice, after a silence of several minutes.
" The eternal God nor punishes, nor blesses
at once, but by degrees, and by warnings.
He hath promised his mercy to them that be
truly repentant, although it be at their latter
end; but he hath not promised to the pre-
sumptuous sinner, either that he shall have long
life, or true repentance at the last end: therefore hath he made every man's death uncertain.
Herein have I executed the will of heaven—
not by special mission, for I am unworthy:
but that in my knowledge of that man's crimes,
I had the will and power thus to punish him.
Marvel not, therefore, at what thou hast
beheld. Of the wretched, he was most
wretched; for there are none so wretched as
they who have a conscience seared. Such a
man builds a wall at his back; he cannot, if
he would, return."

" To shew us what you have," replied De
Clare, " and bid us not wonder, is as incon-

gruous as it would be to place us on the rack,
and say, ' be merry.' But, if ever the wish to
inquire could be stifled by the use of that which
doth stir inquiry, it would be when such a
demi-devil was blotted out of existence."

" He was indeed an incomparable villain,"
observed Walwyn.

" Why, the deeds of his single life," said
Peverell, " were sufficient to furnish the calen-
dar of crimes for a whole century of a well re-
gulated state."

" I protest in all sincerity," said Mortimer,
" I gave him the benefit of as much villainy as
my ripe conceptions of sin would let me : but
his performances outstript my most liberal al-
lowance. He was the devil's abridgment—
Lucifer's copy in little—by my faith, a very
incarnation of Beelzebub !"

" It surprises me now," added De Clare,
" that crossing him as we did, we escaped his
secret but swift revenge. He was one of those
bravos, whom I should have guessed no one

that was not weary of life, would have a difference with, and walk abroad after day-light."

" Except," observed Lacy, " that you ever
find cowardice mated with cruelty."

" Seeing what I have, mark you," said Owen
Rees, " I account myself the richer in honour,
by so much honour, as I should have lost, mark
you, had I enforced satisfaction for the affront
he put upon me.   But it is better sometimes
to have a knave's contumely than his blood.
Well—well—may Heaven forgive him all his
other offences as I do, mark you, his having
called me a mountain goat—mark you !"

" I hope," observed Hungerford Hoskyns,
" the gentleman who has taken charge of our
late friend, will see that he has christian
burial."

" It is a sorry jest," replied Fitz-Maurice,
with an air of serious displeasure, " that lies in
the profaning of things sacred ; as it was a
miserable valour, in him you speak of, to dare
the Almighty.   We are brethren, for nobler

and better purposes. I am here to-night to shew you with what instruments Heaven vouch-safes to work. To-morrow night, if the faith that is plighted, be ransomed, I shall be here to achieve the consummation of all !"

" To-morrow night ?" exclaimed Peverell.

" Even so ;" replied Fitz-Maurice.

" To-morrow night then !" repeated Peverell, in a half whisper to himself, " will be the consummation of all !"

" Of all !" said Fitz-Maurice. " Have *you* any doubts ?"

" None," answered Peverell calmly; " you have said so, and it is enough. But what afterwards ?"

Fitz-Maurice made no reply—Peverell started. A voice, at that moment, breathed gently in his ear—a voice he had heard *once* before, " *Thou fool, why so impatient ? Thou art the last !*" He was silent.

" It would ill beseem me," continued Fitz-Maurice, addressing them collectively, " for any cause, less than the one that sways me singly, and binds me to you all, to breathe the thoughts that now agitate my mind. But we tread close upon the unveiling of these mysteries; and one faltering step, one timid spirit, in the final act, would not alone frustrate all—not alone render valueless, as the dust beneath your feet, all that has been done—but would leave me, and all of you, to a fate, from the bare contemplation of which my soul recoils with horror. Therefore it is, that in this place, and at this hour, I would renew that chivalrous oath of fealty which, three nights since, you took, to watch and fear not, for twice the period you had already done so. By this holy emblem, I swear," he continued (taking up the Jerusalem cross that still lay upon the table before him), " it is not that I doubt your manly spirits to confront whate'er shall shew itself—neither your fidelity in what you stand engaged to do: but *I* have conditions to fulfil —conditions which must not, in their smallest obligation, be infringed. Now, it is known to ye all, that in the self-imposed oath you took—the voluntary league you framed—one among you denied your power, laughed at your compact, and refused to plight his troth. You were not of one voice, therefore, in your pre-determined will, howe'er it might fall, that you were of one purpose, in the execution of it. But, more than all, it was *from* yourselves, and *to* yourselves, the oath proceeded and applied ; for *I* could not then receive, what now I can ; which is, that on *my* sword you swear, for eight-and-forty hours, to hold yourselves my followers. And you must do this with absolute and entire confidence—without question, where-fore I require it,—or reservation whereto it shall compel you."

Fitz-Maurice ceased, and drawing forth his sword, held it out. The blade was a superb Damascus one ; one half exquisitely polished, and the other, up to the hilt, black, and traced

E 2

all over with strange hieroglyphic characters, wrought in gold.

There was a brief pause. At length Peverell arose, and placing his hand upon that part of the sword which bore the mystic inscription, exclaimed, " I swear !" The rest followed his example.

" And now," said Fitz-Maurice, returning the weapon to its scabbard, " there remains but this, and we separate. Heed me well. Hold no communion to-morrow with each other; but let every one so employ the time, as he would in preparation for a great emprise. We are never so well fitted to receive Heaven's best gifts, as when we are ready for its most trying dispensations. He whose sinews are strung for the camel's burden, will not faint beneath the weight of his own. Be each of you companion to his own thoughts only ; and when the sun goes down, be willing, and in a condition, to exclaim—' If thou rise no more for me, thou joyous orb, I mourn not ; for I shall dwell in un-

created light, that was, ere time began, and shall
be, when it is no more!' This is a Christian's
daily death, who therefore never dies, but
passes onward to eternity. At the eleventh
hour of night assemble—not where you have
been wont—but beside the humble grave of
him who first wrestled with this mighty mystery. There will I be! It is meet we now
depart."

Fitz-Maurice rose, and, followed by the rest,
paced along the sounding aisles, which seemed
to echo their footsteps in more than mortal
sounds. Arrived at the door, they found Mephosto waiting with his palfrey, which he instantly mounted, and waving his hand to them,
galloped off, as he exclaimed, " Remember !"

De Clare, Peverell, and the others, walked
slowly along. No one spoke ; and when, sepa-
rating, they bade each other good night, each
man proceeded homewards, with such thoughts
and feelings as had never yet occupied his
mind or heart.

CHAPTER VI.

HELEN had carefully avoided any interview
with her father, during the remainder of the
preceding day, after Fitz-Maurice left her;
and before he returned from the Abbey, she
had retired to her chamber for the night. She
had passed the intermediate hours in weeping
and praying; in silent meditation, and in fruit-
less efforts to penetrate the future.

What most embarrassed and afflicted her, was
the positive injunction of Fitz-Maurice, that

no human being should know of her design on
the following night. It was like condemning
her to severe bodily pain, and forbidding her
to cry out. The enterprise was big with she
knew not what dangers and difficulties, and
she was pitilessly enjoined to brave them all,
by the unsupported energy of her own mind.
This thought almost overpowered her, sometimes ; and she became half resolved to renounce
the performance of her promise, from an idea
that if what had been exacted of her were pure
and holy, it could not need such secresy.

Then, with a trembling hand, she would turn
over the leaves of those books she possessed,
which disclosed all the mysteries of the necromantic art, to see if there were any trials which
others had undergone, or any situations in
which others had been placed, that at all
resembled her own. But she could find none ;
though she discovered much that taught her to
dread the consequences of violating such a compact as she had made. Above all, she feared

that influence of wizard wrath, which might
place knives, or halters, or deadly infusion of
life-destroying herbs, in her path, and so tempt
her, beyond her strength, to horrible self-
murder ! She closed her books, strengthened
rather than weakened in her resolution, to
hazard whatever might happen from the third
display of the signet's potency.

Often did she look upon that mysterious
agent of an invisible and unknown power; and
often did her tears fall upon it, as she darkly
wondered what might be its remaining behest.
At those moments, her thoughts reverted to
her father—to all that Fitz-Maurice had said
—to all that had passed at Margery Ashwell's.

It was her pride and consolation to reflect, in
this crisis of her fate, that no considerations of
what could happen to herself, divided for an
instant, or mingled with, the singleness of her
anxiety for her father's safety. What, indeed,
she felt most bitterly was, that in all she had

done, in all she had suffered, she was still baffled in that for which she had done all, and suffered all. She was not assured that her beloved father's life was beyond the aim of danger. She hoped it was—she believed it was—she strove to torture a meaning out of Fitz-Maurice's words, and out of Alascon's answers, which would warrant both; but still the sickening dread returned upon her, that when it was too late, perhaps, she would find how fondly she had construed every thing. Even the idle roundelay, which the blind minstrel had played, and the blue-eyed girl had sung, came in aid of her worst fears; and she repeated often, with a sorrowful and foreboding • heart,

" But the pang of despair, which was keener than all,
Was the pang of her SOUL for a word past recal."

At other times, she would think with dismay of the closing vision of the magic glass, and, in passionate grief, throw herself upon her knees,

and pray to Heaven that her right arm might
wither, and drop from her, if that hideous
shadow foretold a truth.   In this agony, a ray
of comfort would break forth, in the remembrance that she had beheld herself, coffined and
sepulchred, ere the other appalling phantom
crossed her, and so, perchance, it might be the
emblem of that death which her own would
inflict upon her unhappy father: a thought
infinitely more tolerable than the other.

Nor could she disguise from herself, in this
stormy conflict of contending hopes, and fears,
and wishes, that a prevailing desire ran through
them all—to release Fitz-Maurice, (even at the
price of her own life, if that alone were demanded,) from his destiny, whatever it was:
to do " one deed of heavenly goodness more;"
to give " one closing trial of her faith;" one
" last display of dauntless courage;" to " strike
off his fetters;" to " throw wide open his
prison doors;" to " redeem him from his captivity."

All the feelings with which that mysterious being had first inspired her; all the intense sympathy and ardent pity which he had first awakened in her bosom, had been a hundred fold increased by his last appeal. She imagined, she knew not why, but she was conscious of the impulse (as if it were the highly wrought sense of a great moral and religious duty) that some obligation, which had Heaven for its warranty, some obscurely sacred command, lay upon her to work out his redemption. The most subtle examination of her own heart could detect there no lurking human love—no struggling woman's passion—but solely and entirely an absorbing, overpowering, and pleasing conviction, that she had been born, and had been permitted to live till then, only for the accomplishment of this predestined purpose. No holy virgin, kneeling at the cloistered shrine, and rapt into devout ecstacy, as she dedicated herself, for aye, to the service of Almighty God, ever did so with a more sainted spirit, than did

Helen, at some moments of her solitary meditations, consecrate herself the " bride of Christ,"
when, in imagination, she was crying aloud at
the Abbey door, " Husband, come ! the cross
is mine !"

Thus passed the hours of solitude to which
she had consigned herself, alternately the sport
of earthly fears and of heavenly hopes ; now,
beset with mortal apprehensions—now, soaring,
with enthusiastic spirit, into visionary worlds—
at one moment, shrinking with all her sex's
fearfulness from danger, and at the next, glowing with all a martyr's zeal, stedfast in the truth.
Filial love, pious obedience, and natural misgivings, besieged her heart in quick succession.
The first and last distressed it ; the second only
seemed to subdue its anguish.   She dwelt upon
it, therefore, more frequently, and every time
with increasing fervour.

As often as she regarded herself called to this
sharp trial, by the darkly revealed will of God ;
as often as she saw, in her prescribed task,

only the fulfilling of his mandate, all doubt
and terror vanished. There was then no link
in her thoughts which connected them with
this earth. They partook of that sanctity
which elevates things temporal to things spi-
ritual, and transformed what was required of
her, from a dubious duty to a sacred obla-
tion.

It was no wonder, therefore, that, in the end,
she gradually and insensibly, almost, clung to
this belief; that she banished alike from her
mind those hopes and fears which she could
neither confirm nor remove; and that she endeavoured to repose, calmly and meekly, upon the
assurance of a pre-ordained mission of holiness.
It was with this strong persuasion, created in
her after a long and severe self-struggle, that
she retired to her pillow. But the subject of
her waking meditations weaved itself into the
shadowy texture of her dreams; and her slum-
bering fancy beguiled her with vain shows,

which she recalled with a more than supersti-
tious confidence in what they foreboded.

She dreamed she was a living witness of that
great work of redemption wrought for us, by
the infinite mercy and goodness of Him, who
was crucified. She stood, in the valley of
carcases, at the foot of Mount Calvary, and
beheld that perfect example and pattern of all
meekness and sufferance, led forth to his most
vile and slanderous death ! She saw his blessed
body hanging upon the cross, his head covered
with sharp thorns, his hands and feet wounded
with nails, his side pierced with a long spear,
his flesh rent and torn with whips, his brows
sweating water and blood ; and she felt the
earth quake beneath her feet, and saw the
stones cleave asunder—and the graves open,
and the dead bodies rise. While gazing with
intolerable agony and dismay upon this awful
scene, she thought an aged man who stood
beside her, wailing and lamenting in deep tri-
bulation, exclaimed, " Daughter ! take heed

to thyself and to thy soul, with all carefulness, lest thou forgettest the things which thine eyes have seen." And she said, " Why, oh father! speakest thou this?" And he replied, " That thou mayest know, in the time to come, wherefore thou wert born." And she thought it *was* her father who spake to her: but at that moment, and ere she could answer again, the multitude raised a loud shout; and were violently agitated to and fro; and with the tumult and noise, she awoke.

At any other time, and with a mind less disturbed, Helen would have regarded this vision of her sleep as the natural consequence, and nothing more, of the reflections which had engrossed her thoughts during the day. But now, it was no idle dream; no airy phantasm of the brain, wildly sporting at will, while reason slumbered, and delusively clothing itself in the very shape and seeming which her own sick heart had imaged; but an actual and solemn manifestation, by divine agency, of the

thing she was to do. She found, indeed, an
infinite relief in the persuasion that her path
was now distinctly pointed out, and that she
need no longer perplex herself with vain en-
deavours to discover it. Clouds and shadows
still rested upon it in the distance : she could
not see beyond them : she knew not why she was
to tempt them, but she was prepared to do so, and
found herself mistress of sufficient fortitude, as she
firmly believed, to abide whatever might follow

Lacy sought an interview with Helen soon
after she had risen, on the following morning,
and while she was still pondering on all the
circumstances connected with her enterprise,
and with her dream of the preceding night.
He, too, had anxiously revolved in his thoughts,
the extraordinary fate of Wilfrid Overbury, and
the earnest desire of Fitz-Maurice that they
should renew their oath to himself; as well as
the reasons he assigned for requiring that new
covenant, and above all, the emphatic language he had addressed to them when direct-

ing that they should assemble the next night
at the grave of Kit Barnes. But he possessed
an elasticity of character which soon recovered
itself from the pressure of events. It had
been the business of his life, to act rather than
to think; to perform what was to be done,
rather than to inquire too curiously the cause;
and to pass, with rapidity, from one under-
taking to another. He possessed, also, what
is a very common consequence of such habits,
a fondness for the excitement produced by a
quick succession of hazardous situations; and
most certainly, he looked forward to the final
developement of all the strange scenes in which
he had been recently engaged, with more of
impatient curiosity than of fear or reluctance.

CHAPTER VII.

WHEN Helen entered the room in which her
father was sitting, he was struck with her altered
appearance. It was not that she looked care-
worn; or that her eyes were inflamed with
weeping; or that her air was languid from sickness; or that the weariness of a restless night
hung about her. A deep gloom overspread her
pallid countenance; a determined energy was
imprinted on every feature. Her eye was cold
and resolute; her brow was knit, as if the mind
within were ruminating upon some great design
whose secret character none might penetrate;

and about her slightly quivering lips played an
exulting expression, partaking equally of conscious firmness and half revealed fear. Her
voice, too, was mournfully tender, giving forth
those calm, dejected tones, which speak the
feelings of a heart that sorrows without hope;
while her whole deportment denoted the hard
fought victory of a gentle spirit warring with
itself, and twining with its sad laurels, the
sadder cypress wreath.

She read in her father's looks, all that he would
have spoken. She knew, full well, they were
but the reflection of her own; but she felt it was
no time for soft words or bland endearments;
and the effort she made to repel their approach
only imparted an increased sternness to her
manner.

" I am your Helen, still," said she, (as Lacy
took her hand, and gazed in her face with that
silent grief which never yet found words to tell
itself—the prophetic grief of an adoring heart,
that sees, or fancies it sees, death's pale sum-

mons on the cheek it loves)—" I am your Helen still, only less happy, perchance, than I have been wont. But smiles will come again, when hope, like returning spring, shall scatter her fresh flowers over my now wintry mind."

Lacy pressed her hand, and turned aside his head, to conceal the tears which he could not command back.

" What happened last night ?" continued Helen calmly.

" In the Abbey, do you mean ?" said Lacy, with a tremulous voice, seating himself in a chair, with his face still averted.

" Yes," replied Helen, " in the Abbey. Was Fitz-Maurice there ?"

" He was," answered Lacy.

" And," added Helen, after a pause, while seating herself by her father's side, " what said he ? what did he ? or rather, what was done ?"

" Why should I distress you further in this business ?" said he. " Do I not perceive how fatally the knowledge of it has already worked ?

Do I not know, even from your own lips, that
it hath engulphed you in its vortex? The
unexplained mystery of your chain and cross,
(which, observe, I seek not to penetrate, but
wait till you see the fit time for divulging,)
informs me, too certainly, that in some way or
other you have, for my sake, connected yourself with these dark events. I cannot, perhaps,
undo the past; but I may be able to avoid
augmenting the perils of the future."

"Why then, I am denied," answered Helen,
"to partake with you the perils you admit.
And why? Because you think I am too much
woman to bear their onset. Indeed, indeed,
if you knew all, if you *could* know all, I should
be the chosen sharer of your secrets; and not
their rejected seeker."

"If I *could* know all!" exclaimed Lacy,
"what is it you mean?"

"That you should think me, as you have
ever found me," replied Helen, "worthy of
your confidence. This may seem high lan-

guage from a daughter; but in sooth, it is from
no bold, immodest spirit, that I speak thus. In
all, save this, I own a becoming obedience to
thy will; in nought, save this, should I trust
myself with nay, when thou hadst said aye."

Lacy was subdued: not more by the gentle
submission of this appeal, than by the repose
of Helen's manner, which breathed the serenity
of a mind settled to some great purpose, from
which no ordinary impediments could divert it,
and which evidently sought the information it
would have, not to guide or determine its
course, (for that was fixed beyond changing,)
but to possess a full knowledge, if possible, of
all that might avail to make it efficacious. He,
therefore, no longer hesitated to relate the oc-
currences of the preceding night, to the whole
of which Helen listened with deep attention.
She evinced much horror, at the recital of
Overbury's crimes, and astonishment at the
visible representation of them on board the
Scorpion; seemed surprised at the renewal of

their oaths towards Fitz-Maurice, and could hardly conceal her agitation when she heard where they were to assemble that night. She made her father repeat, more than once, the very words used by Fitz-Maurice in enjoining them to hold no communion with each other during the day, and dwelt, with apparent anxiety, upon his declaration, that they were treading close upon the unveiling of all these mysteries.

"What he meant," observed Lacy, "by saying 'it has not been always thus, and would not be so now, but for thee and thine,' when that ugly dwarf came crouching to his feet, I know not. I have no skill in riddles; and his answer to me about the dawn, and the traveller, the landscape, and sun rise, was a riddle, and nothing better, to my apprehension."

"It was his purpose," replied Helen, "so to veil his meaning, that it should not be read with too large or particular an understanding of its aim. But—"

She paused ; and then suddenly changed the subject of conversation, by exclaiming, " And *you* go to the Abbey this night at *eleven* o'clock ?"

" At that hour Fitz-Maurice is to be with us," replied Lacy, " but *I* do not go alone, as you seem to imagine."

" No, no ;" said Helen, " you will all be there—all—I know—to witness greater wonders than any you have yet beheld. I am no prophetess—no Cassandra—but I pronounce truths that shall be : and you, my father—you, more than all, shall be moved with astonishment !"

" How know *you* this ?" inquired Lacy.

" Do you remember yesterday, and ask ?" replied Helen.

" I do remember yesterday, and ask," said Lacy ; " for I have not, till now, seen you since your interview with Fitz-Maurice. What passed between you ?"

" A wild and wondrous scene," answered

Helen, "befitting the occasion ; and the—man, I was about to say—but if he be man only, all *other* men are less than what they seem."

"Is it so !" exclaimed her father, significantly.

"Fie upon that thought !" retorted Helen : "It wrongs me. Have you ever seen me so lightly enamoured, or witnessed so loose an affection in me, as to warrant the construction you have put upon my words ? But this is no moment for vain discourse. In sooth, it *was* a wild and wondrous scene ; for amazement, pity, and almost madness, followed each word he spoke. I am not prone to weep ; nor think there's witchcraft in a maiden's tears ; but I wept, to hear a tale so sad as his ; and still the more I wept, as I learned how only the griefs that thronged upon him could be shaken off !"

"And how, my child," said Lacy, "can they be shaken off ? If, by any honourable means, that lie not beyond me, I swear, were it only that in thy gentle heart they have awakened compassion, he might freely command my ut-most."

" I know not," replied Helen, " what giant's strength it may have required to forge and rivet the fetters that gall him ; but a very pigmy's will suffice to strike them loose. There needs no martial hand like thine."

" Whose, then ?" inquired her father.

" Mine !" responded Helen.

" Yours !" exclaimed Lacy, " I cannot com-prehend you—I could almost add, I fear to do so. To what hath he obtained your con-sent ?"

" To two things," said Helen.

" Name them," replied her father.

" The first, a solemn vow of SILENCE," an-swered Helen, emphatically.

" The second—" continued Lacy,

" Is in the holy keeping of that solemn vow," added Helen.

" Nay, now methinks, you do but trifle with my anxious cares for thee," said her father, in a tone that was half reproachful. "I do not lay my injunctions upon you, because it is only with rugged and ungentle natures that such rough authority is needful; but if you are, indeed, as you have said, my Helen still, you will be like yourself, and lay your heart before me as you have ever done. Reflect a moment, my dear child, and you will acknowledge your present situation to be one, which stands in need of riper counsel than your green years can offer. If you have too unwisely bound yourself to the performance of an act, or difficult, or dangerous to perform, reveal its quality, and my matured experience may find such honourable releases from it, as might never suggest themselves to your unpractised mind. Even were it otherwise, and that whate'er you intend must perforce be executed, still let not me be a stranger to it. For too well, I note, in thy much altered appearance, in thy sadness of speech, and in that breaking face, which foretells a breaking heart, that some heavy mischance, some grievous trou-

ble afflicts you.   Helen ! you have no mother !
If you had,—if that pattern of all gentleness and
love were now upon earth, and could take you
to her arms; if she could hang over you, and
with her tears, her prayers, win you to confession—if you had her kind, maternal bosom to
receive you, her endearing accents to comfort
you, her watchful care to guard you from all
danger—I should not, as now I do, vex you
with my importunities.   But fancy it is your
mother speaks in me, for sure I am, that could
her voice pierce the tomb, it would not entreat
you with a holier or a warmer love than mine !"

The tremulous tone with which Lacy uttered
these last words, and the tender earnestness of
his manner before, quite overpowered Helen.
The mention of her mother, thrilled to her heart,
and awakened bitter anguish at the thought
that in this arduous crisis of her fate, she was,
indeed, without the consolation which her presence would have imparted.   But she roused
herself from the enervating reflection—repelled

the emotions which were kindling in her bosom, drove back the gathering tears that would soon have fallen else, from her eyes, and with a determined effort to maintain the unbending firmness which she well knew could, alone, carry her through the terrible trial that awaited her, she addressed her father.

" I am too strongly grafted in your opinion," said she, " to require that I should affirm, it is no proud temper, or moody humour, which makes me withhold instant obedience to your will. I cannot, I must not, speak; yet, judge by what I am about to declare, that a powerful necessity constrains me to conceal a part. You have no faith in that, which I most devoutly believe,—that, for purposes inscrutable to us, the Almighty hath ever permitted, and doth still permit, wizards and magicians, and charmers, and necromancers, to exercise strange powers over the operations of nature; to know the future; and by subtle enchantments, to influence the events of this world. Why, else, are we admonished of such things, in the sacred homilies delivered in our churches, and taught to pray for deliverance from the evils which they can inflict upon us? But is it not in daily proof that what I say is true? All men do not believe so, you will reply; and my answer is, that all men do not believe in Christ crucified. But shall they whose faith is lively in the cross, renounce it, because paynims and Jews deny our blessed Redeemer? You will not wonder then, my dear father, having told you I devoutly believe in the intermediate agency of these mysterious beings, that, seeing what hath taken place in our venerable Abbey, and filled with insupportable fears for thy safety, I have sought to obtain, by means like those which I deemed had encompassed you with danger, a power to save you."

" Gracious Heaven !" exclaimed Lacy, " you have not, surely, invoked the dark spirits of the abyss, or subdued them to your will, by any of those damning spells and sorceries which I have heard of ?"

"How could I do so," replied Helen, with a smile, "if, as your creed is, there are no such dark spirits, no such spells, no such sorceries ?"

"True," said her father, "but I may be wrong ; and in the bare possibility that I am, lies a tremendous consequence, if, in your knowledge of the truth, you have employed them to your soul's perdition."

"Heaven forefend," exclaimed Helen, "that for any earthly good I should barter away eternal felicity ! No ! I love you with a sufficient devotion, and prize your life and happiness enough to offer my own for them ; to exchange for them my all of worldly hope : but I love my God more, and prize his approving smile beyond all the temptations that could make me forfeit it !"

"There spoke my own Helen !" said Lacy, pressing her hand affectionately—"there the sainted nature of thy mother shone brightly forth !

Well, my child : thus relieved, I think I can
calmly hear all that thou hast to say more."

" It is but little," rejoined Helen. " I *have*
employed, and holily employed, in all that
concerns myself, for I sought my object
through the cunning skill of others, those
necromantic arts by which the future is unveiled to mortal eyes. Nor have I employed
them vainly. I am amazed there should dwell
that look of doubt upon your face. Can you
remember what you have yourself seen,—can
you remember the finding of my cross and chain,
with the mystic scroll floating in the former—
and still refuse to believe that they are not all
natural ? Methinks, if I could tell you yet a
little more than what thou hast already seen,
those doubts would for ever vanish. But this
I may not. What I have learned, is for mine
own heart to know, not for my tongue to utter.
And my hopes are fervent, that at the appointed
time, all the sufferings I have endured, all the
trials I have sustained, will yield a rich harvest

in the power I shall have to protect you, should perils circumvent you. Fitz-Maurice is now your avowed leader in this great business ; for great it is, and holy too, I do believe ! Heed him well ; I speak it not lightly or fantastically, when I say he is the champion of a sacred cause, howe'er it may also appear that he hath been captive to a sinful and impure spirit. Oh, my father ! ere yon sun shall shine again where now it does, my lips will be unsealed, all mystery will depart from me, and thou, like a good and faithful soldier to the last, shall return with honour to thy once more peaceful home !"

" That I shall be the last, or among the last, to quit this enterprise," said Lacy, " is most true. For though I began it with a fickle purpose, scarcely resolved, from hour to hour, whether to stop, or go on, I am now too deeply engaged, both by my plighted honour to others, and my cares for thee, to renounce it. But I shall wear a heavy heart to-night ! I know not

why it should be so, more than last night, for
then my thoughts were full of you, and
gloomier withal, in that I was less acquainted
with the nature of the thing I feared. It
might serve to enforce a preacher's text upon
the uncertainty of life, if I, who have sought
death in every dangerous path, in the listed
field, in foreign climes, mid shouting squadrons,
and on the midnight watch, should find him at
last, like a lazy citizen at home, who is knocked
on the head in some street brawl !"

" I pray you, talk not thus," said Helen,
" or I shall lose confidence in myself, and mar
I know not what, by forsaking my intentions.
But why do you fear the issue of this night's
business ?"

" I will not call it fear," replied Lacy, " but
a foreboding sadness, which I can well believe,
I should not have, wert thou clear of all participation in our proceedings."

" Oh ! banish that augury," answered Helen,
" if there be nothing more to warrant your

sadness. Did Fitz-Maurice, when he appointed the hour of eleven to meet him, speak of twelve ?"

" Of twelve !" responded Lacy.

" Aye," continued Helen, " of the hour of twelve ?"

" No," replied her father. " I have told you, with what exactness my memory would let me, the whole that passed."

" Then," said Helen, " *I* bid you be prepared for that hour."

" Why ?"

" That," said she, " the hour itself must tell : but watch ! And now," she continued, rising from her seat, " it would refresh my wearied spirit to walk awhile—the air is cool and the sun bright. His cheerful beams will dispel the clouds that have gathered over us."

CHAPTER VIII.

HELEN was desirous of terminating a conversation which she felt could continue no
longer, without becoming every moment more
and more embarrassing.   She had disclosed all
she could : all, indeed, she wished at that time ;
and she knew she had touched the verge, the
brink of all she dare, in directing her father's
attention to the hour when she herself should
appear in the Abbey ; while the having done so
would inevitably have led to further questions
on his part.   Therefore it was that she proposed to go forth upon the terrace; a propo-

sition to which Lacy readily assented; and
during their walk she studiously contrived to
keep him in conversation upon every subject
but the one which had hitherto been the theme
of their discourse. On their return to the
house, Helen retired immediately to her own
chamber; where she continued for several
hours alone, still absorbed in meditation upon
the task she had to perform, and which as the
time drew near, presented itself to her imagination under a thousand different aspects.

She was sitting at her window, pensively
watching the declining sun, and thinking
whether she should ever again look upon its
departing glories, when little Bridget entered
her room, with a visible expression of alarm
upon her countenance. She pointed to the
door, and exclaimed, " Don't be frightened—
she's coming :" and before Helen could inquire
who was coming, she saw the decrepit form of
Margery Ashwell limping towards her, leaning
on the black twisted crutch, whose trans-

formation to a living reptile had so terrified her, on the night of the incantation.

Helen could not repress a slight tremor, which ran through her shivering frame, as she looked at the beldam, and remembered with what malignant fury she had threatened her, when the agony of her feelings prevented her from speaking to the spirit which, with such powerful charms, she had evoked. As to poor little Bridget, the drifted snow is not more colourless than were her cheeks and lips; and when a look from Helen told her she was to leave the chamber, she did so without the use of her eyes; for not once did she take them off Margery, till she had the door in her hand, and then she directed one beseeching and pity-ing glance towards her mistress, as if she would have said, in her own emphatic brevity of speech, " don't trust her ! God help you !"

Helen, however, had recovered from the first feeling of trepidation excited by this unex-pected visit, and kindly placed a chair for the

withered crone, who seated herself in it with a
"Heigho!" as if she were sorely fatigued by
her walk.

"It is a weary distance," said she, "for my
old limbs! And I made the distance greater,
by coming through the church-yard, and down
the green lane, at the back of the Abbey, to
avoid the rabblement; for when they see me in
the town, they call me witch, and set young
urchins to pinch me; and the wenches will
leave their spinning, to come and tear my
flesh, till they see blood. Hang them! I
harm them not, though not a mischief happens to
child or mother, cattle or house, but it is of my
doing! So I keep the field, and the heath,
and the lone path, and steal abroad at this
still hour of evening, when the owl wakes for
the night, and the glow-worm trims his lamp
by the last beam of the setting sun."

Helen did not venture to interrupt her during this soliloquy, but waited till she should,
herself, and after her own manner, declare the

object of her visit. The beldam, however, seemed in no hurry to do so; for she now sat, muttering to herself in half words and sentences, while her sharp grey eyes wandered wildly round the apartment, noting all that it contained; and sometimes their penetrating look was fixed upon Helen. In one corner hung a virginal, which seemed particularly to attract her attention; whether it was that she knew not its use, or that it attracted her more frequent notice, because immediately above it was suspended a finely executed portrait of Helen's mother, painted shortly after her marriage; and round her neck she wore the very chain and cross which Helen had entrusted to her keeping the morning she first sought her cottage. There was, too, so striking a resemblance between Helen and her mother, as the latter appeared when this likeness was taken, except in the colour of the hair, that the picture might almost have passed for a portrait of herself. After some time, she again addressed Helen.

" You came to me," said she, " in doubt and trouble, and I did my best to relieve both; but had I known the potent spell you bore about you, I could have done much more. You should have had Hecate herself to answer you, though you had demanded to know the charm by which she puts the darkened moon into an eclipse."

" I heard and saw enough," said Helen, shuddering at the recollection of the scene.

" I was never so bestraught," continued the hag, " as when I saw your fair hand stretched forth, and heard you pronounce those compelling words. But that is past. You swooned, or —"

" Or what?" exclaimed Helen, eagerly, perceiving that Margery hesitated.

" Alascon had shewn you ANOTHER vision, worth all the rest !"

" What was it?" said Helen. " Did you see it ?"

" Aye !" replied Margery, with a sigh.

" What was it ?" repeated Helen : " tell me !"

" By the pit of Acheron, I dare not," she replied. " My tongue would wither, and become like the blasted bough of a thunder-stricken tree, if it spoke of what the eye alone should see."

A pause ensued. The hag sat rocking to and fro, her two hands leaning upon her crutch, and guttural sounds, that scarcely took the shape of words, issuing from her lips. Helen, opposite to her, her pale face lighted up with the flush cast upon it by the crimson effulgence of the westering sun, her cheek supported by her delicately formed hand, and her full dark eyes bent upon the ground ; while busy thought was calling forth image after image, as her fancy strove to picture what might have been the unseen vision of Alascon's mirror, that was worth all the rest. How beautifully were contrasted, at that moment, her youthful figure, her pensive features, and her sun-illumined brow of alabaster, with the aged form, palsied limbs, and wrinkled face of Margery Ashwell, dimly visible in the thickening gloom of the shadows of evening!

Helen, now slowly raised her head, and looking at Margery, "Though," said she, "you dare not tell me what my heart yearns to know, you can disclose, perhaps, that which took place after I became insensible."

"That can I, and that may I," exclaimed Margery, starting up, as if from a profound reverie; "and that will I too! There shall be many a gentle maiden perplexed as thou art, ere there shall be another favoured as thou art. Thou cam'st in the dark hour of midnight to my cottage, and yet I trow thy shoon were not wet with the dank grass, nor thy dainty feet weary with the many steps I have trod to come hither. Ah, well-a-day!—it was a sight, I ween, to make an old heart leap for joy, to see how thou wast no sooner down in sorrow than raised in comfort, and, like a nursling in its mother's arms, borne away, tramp! tramp! on the swift steed of the BLACK HORSEMAN."

" The Black Horseman!" exclaimed Helen.

" Aye," said Margery. " The flesh lights were yet burning as he entered, and e'en as I would pick up a feather, he lifted you from the earth and sprung with you into his saddle."

" You mean,"—replied Helen, with a faltering voice,—" you mean Fitz-Maurice."

" I mean the BLACK HORSEMAN," said Margery; " call you him, Fitz-Maurice, or any name you list—He, who rides the world by day, and by night, and will to the Holy Land and back again, while a cloud, no bigger than my hand, sails across the moon—he, who gallops over steeples, if a church-yard lie in his way, because a mightier one than himself hath put him under the ban of never finding a grave! It is upon his errand I am here; and beshrew me, I have prated so long, that the twilight will be gone, ere I perform it."

Helen was unable to speak ; the designation

which Margery had given to Fitz-Maurice astonished her; and her blood ran chill as she thought of it.

" Here," continued Margery Ashwell, as she drew from beneath her cloak, an oblong ebony box, which had been fastened to her side by a leathern strap, " here is what you will need to-night."

She laid the box upon the ground, opened it, and took out a long white veil and a bridal garment.

" How is this ?" exclaimed Helen, with increasing agitation and surprise.

" It is for you," said Margery.

" For me ! And from whom ?" replied Helen.

" You need not ask from whom, or for what," muttered the beldam. " Whither thou goest to-night, thou canst not go except it be with this gear on thee. Why, what a coil is here, forsooth !—I tell thee again, there shall be many a gentle maiden perplexed as thou art, ere there shall be another favoured as thou art. I would be thy tire-woman, and array thee in this robe of gladness, but that my son, my delicate Hopdance, hath the knotted cramp, and moans for my return. And here," continued Margery, holding up a small silken bag, "here is that which, hung round thy ivory neck, shall make thee walk unseen amid the gaze of a thousand eyes; as every shamefast virgin would fain do at her espousal. This is the wondrous herb that bears no flower; whose quick conceiving seed engendereth in a single night; 'twas gathered by myself, after many a weary watching. Rustic maidens call it fern seed; and whoso carries it near her heart, and wills that it should work, is straight invisible to mortal sight."

Helen surveyed, with an aching heart, the things that were spread before her; but ere she could again address herself to Margery, the ancient dame had hobbled to the door, and holding up her crutch exclaimed, as she quitted the room, "Rejoice, that thine hour of deliverance is nigh."

" Rejoice !" she repeated to herself, and sunk into silent meditation. Her mind, which had assumed something like composure, was now again unbalanced. She could not dismiss from it the thought of the *black horseman*, which seemed to convey a notion of Fitz-Maurice, far different from any she had yet entertained respecting him. It was doubtless he, and no one else, who had conveyed her out of the cottage. Yet it might have been some spirit of darkness ! But that was impossible, for the bridal garments that lay at her feet, could have come only from Fitz-Maurice, for only he knew the use that was to be made of them. She was thus wandering from conjecture to conjecture, when she heard the steps of Bridget approaching ; and she hastily concealed the ebony box with its contents, as her faithful domestic entered with lights. Helen found a relief in her unobstrusive conversation, and permitted her to remain ; but she carefully evaded every allusion to the object of Margery Ashwell's visit.

CHAPTER IX.

Lacy and his daughter were not the only
two who looked forward, with an anxious mind,
to the coming night. The address of Fitz-
Maurice had left a vivid impression upon all ;
and though they strictly observed his injunction to have no communion with each other
during the day, the grounds of that injunction,
added to the extraordinary circumstances of
Overbury's fate, and the solemn place appointed for their next meeting, incessantly occupied their thoughts.

Peverell grasped the subject with that singleness of resolution which had marked his conduct throughout. The same determined feeling which made him ride up to the Abbey walls, on the night when he and Clayton were returning from Dunstable, to know *what* it was they had seen, now animated him, to know what was to be the end of all they had seen. There was neither ostentation nor frivolity in his motives. Chance had thrown a difficulty in his way ; and a naturally cool and persevering character impelled him to surmount it. Having fully satisfied himself upon one point, that there was a something to find out, he was content steadily to follow the path which promised to conduct him to the object of his search. It was true, there had been some circumstances, in the progress of the business, which identified him with it, more than any of the rest ; but it was not therefore that his purpose had been so uniform. He was like a man who had begun to ascend a lofty hill ; every step he took, while it brought him nearer to its summit, made him less and less inclined to retrace his ground.

De Clare, on the contrary, who had commenced the inquiry in scorn, almost, and had struggled, more than once, with the proud impatience of his nature, which could not brook to be baffled in its aim, now pursued it with a sort of angry humour, as if he sought to propitiate himself, by finding, at the end, something which should vindicate the beginning. It is doubtful, however, whether any thing short of that pact of honour, which had united him first with his associates, and bound him afterwards to Fitz-Maurice, would have held him to the last : for he delighted to walk alone —to be followed rather than to follow—and to survey, with a scoffing spirit, the busy turmoil of that world from which he disdainfully kept aloof. Something, indeed, was to be ascribed to the influence of Fitz-Maurice, whose absolute and mysterious manner swayed De Clare in spite of himself. He could not sound the depth of his character as he could that of other men ; and although there was a lurking proneness in his bosom, sometimes, to dethrone him from his supremacy, he always found it impossible to do so. Still less possible was it after the events of the preceding night ; and it was even with an unrepining acquiescence, that he submitted to the mandate of abstaining from all intercourse with the rest during that day. " This man hath something in him !" he would exclaim. " He is marked out from the common herd ; and it is not altogether an inglorious bondage to be fettered by his authority. By Heavens ! I hardly think I could carry it myself with a more brave and noble front, against such a heady current of difficulties !" This last consideration mainly contributed to reconcile him with himself.

The choleric Welshman, who would have fought his way out of peril like a lion, but who would seek peril only as an alternative, where the choice lay between bad and worse,

breathed more than one wish, after quitting the
Abbey the preceding night, that he had never
entered it.   He was one of those who thought,
with the adage, that it is best to have a long
spoon when you eat with the devil.   Hitherto
he had been a watcher, with no other fear than
what might be produced by the events of each
night; and he had courage enough to draw his
chance in the lottery of danger.   But he now
began to feel that it was quite another thing to
go and receive his warrant, as it were, for his
individual and allotted portion of the general
hazard.   It was the difference, in his estima-
tion, between being one of many in a fray,
where accidents *might* happen, and thrusting
his head into a furnace, where a miracle *must*
happen, if he got it out again.   So, at least,
he interpreted the language of Fitz-Maurice:
and with such misgiving did he look forward
to the night that was approaching.   Yet,
though he would have given, at that moment,
half his remaining time to live, had he never

seen the Abbey at all, he would not have
accepted a release from whatever was to come,
at the price of a single hair plucked from his
beard.   He was no coward : he was a stranger
to that pale passion : but he lacked the energy
of mind which enables a man to confront calmly
the peril he can dare intrepidly.

As to Hungerford Hoskyns, he troubled
himself no further with the business, than just
to remember that he was to find his way, by
eleven o'clock, to the grave of Kit Barnes.
Come what might, it would come unheeded.
His mind was like the waves of the sea, which
divide themselves beneath the passing keel,
and close again in the same instant. It received
every impression, but retained none. To his
thoughts it could scarcely be said there be-
longed either a past or a future : for the former
was obliterated every moment, and the latter
was incessantly absorbed in the present. If
any one had asked him what *had* taken place
in the Abbey, it would have confounded him

as much as if he had been required to tell what
he dreamed of that day three years; and if
he had asked himself what *was* to take place,
he would have looked at the sky, and, with a
laugh, exclaimed, " Can I tell whether the sun
will shine at twelve o'clock next Christmas
day? No, verily. But when Christmas
comes, we shall all know if it does."

Walwyn had no leisure, from his grief for
the death of Vehan, to perplex himself much
with the approaching issue of the enterprise.
Nor would he have considered it too nicely,
had it been otherwise, after having deliberately
consented to follow it so far. He was one of
those men, in whose nature reason is so pre-
dominant, that he would hardly change the
colour of his cloak, or walk to the right, instead
of to the left, without having first satisfied his
mind as to his own motives. He never shot
his arrow to fall where it might, but always
had an aim, near or distant, great or little.
In this business, he considered it incumbent

upon him, when it was first bruited about, to lend the authority of his countenance, (as one whose station and wealth gave him influence,) to whatever measures should be deemed necessary for subjecting it to a satisfactory investigation. Hence it was, that he sent in his name to the mayor: hence, too, he had continued his attendance: and hence he was resolved to co-operate in bringing it to a conclusion, though the disaster of his kinsman's death had blunted the keenness of the interest he had hitherto felt.

The perfumed gallant, Nicholas Mortimer, had bestowed five minutes of very serious consideration upon the affair, while offering up his morning prayers to his glass, and devoutly imploring that he might be spared the fate of Narcissus. " I protest by my manhood !" he exclaimed, " I will go to this ugly rendezvous in the church-yard ; but I protest, no less, by this glossy curl that so becomes my lip, it were a shame to cry out upon, if that Monsieur

Fitz-Maurice, with his invisible rapier, should
serve me as he did our late friend, the sea-
monster ; for

> " Tell me, thou earthen vessel, made of clay,
> What beauty's worth, if thou must die to-day ?"

But Nicholas Mortimer talked of death, as
lusty youth moralizes upon grey hairs, with
an exulting consciousness of the years that lie
between the discourse and its subject. With
all his outside foppery, he had manliness within;
and upon any trial to which he might be put,
he would have proved that when he swore by
his manhood, he swore by that he had. He
was like a good book with a soiled title-page—
his first leaf was his worst. Turn that over, and
the inside had wherewithal to recommend
itself.

Thus did each, in his own retirement, meditate upon the singular prohibition which lay
upon all, not to have mutual communication.
Meanwhile, the hours glided on, and Peverell

was sitting, musing in his chamber, as the afternoon wore away, when his man Francis entered, and announced a stranger, who would not communicate his name. Peverell had scarcely heard the tidings, when a person appeared before him, habited in a foreign garb. His stature was of the middle height; his air, courteous and unembarrassed; his countenance very pale, and his look, altogether, wan and haggard. He stood for a moment, and eyed Peverell with a calm steady gaze, as if he were debating with himself, whether he was the individual he sought. Peverell at length addressed him.

"I crave your name," said he, pointing to a chair, which the stranger immediately occupied.

"I crave yours," replied the stranger, in a gentle tone of voice.

"Marmaduke Peverell," was the answer.

"And mine, Conrad Geister," said the stranger.

" May I crave your business, too ?" added Peverell.

" It is with you, Marmaduke Peverell," answered Conrad.

" Impart it," said Peverell; " I am ready to hear."

" So shalt thou be to thank me, when thou dost hear.   I come to save thee."

" To save me !" repeated Peverell, "from what, or from whom ?"

" From him who *calls* himself Fitz-Maurice," replied Geister ; " who is—but no matter for that.   Enough for what I seek, that we both mean the same."

" I know Fitz-Maurice," said Peverell.

" And *I* know him," interrupted Geister, " when in the frozen regions of the north, in the mountains and vallies of Scandinavia, he prowled for blood.   I will be frank with you, Marmaduke Peverell, and so merit your confidence   It is for no love I bear you, that I

am here. Why should it? I know you not;
but it is for the hate I bear Fitz-Maurice."

" He has wronged you then?" said Peverell.

" Such deadly wrong," continued Geister,
" as he should have answered with a hundred
lives, if he had had them; or with the one he
has, were he vulnerable to mortal weapon; but
he is armed in devilish sorcery."

" It may be so," replied Peverell; " but it
hath been by other means he hath prevailed
with me."

" Doubtless !" retorted Geister, with a sar-
castic smile. " He hath a glozing tongue,
a pregnant wit, and an admirable carriage.
He can talk smoothly, cozen men with ambi-
guous phrases; play the Delphic god, with
oracular responses; and prate like a cardinal
about things holy. It is thus he makes the
fools of the world his prey. But are you so
dull or so credulous, that you will let this
demi-devil lead you hood-winked to the edge

of the precipice, and mock at you as you topple over?"

" Your pardon," said Peverell; " but when I know better who you are, why you have sought me out, and what you can urge, in honesty and fairness, against Fitz-Maurice, I may listen to you. At present you but waste your breath. I will be as frank with you as you have been with me. You tell me it is hatred of Fitz-Maurice that prompts you in what you do. I will take no man's character from the lips of his avowed enemy."

" Will you take it from your own?" asked Geister.

" What do you mean?" replied Peverell.

" Has he not," continued Geister, with an impassioned energy of manner, " led you on, step by step, till you find yourself enthralled, almost beyond the hope of release? Came he not to you, while yet your resolution was young, and supplied you with seeming reasons why it should wax in strength and form? Sat he not

with you, the first night, in yonder Abbey?
Did he not appear again among you, when your
spirits drooped, and your purpose languished?
Hath he not stirred you to bind yourselves to
each other by an oath? And are you not now
sworn to him by a second oath? And for what
have ye done all this?—To feed your church-
yards! Now, Marmaduke Peverell, answer me
these questions, as ye must, and then, I say, from
your own lips you may take the character of
this Fitz-Maurice. Judge, too, from the knowledge they betray of what hath taken place,
whether it concern you much to know who I
am, further than that I am the enemy of your
enemy?"

"I might answer all your questions," said Peverell, "in the affirmative, and yet be ignorant
how they prove Fitz-Maurice mine enemy. If
you come but to tell me what I know, how
shall your errand prosper? If you have that to
tell me which I do not know, the success of
your errand must still lie in the quality of your

information. I am not so fantastical, to demo-
lish my opinion with the self-same reasons that
I built it up. But will you answer *me* a plain
question ?"

" Ask it," said Geister.

" How have you become possessed of the
knowledge you have, respecting Fitz-Maurice
and myself ?"

" I will *not* answer you," replied Geister.

" Then," added Peverell, " have you aught
else with me? If not, I have other and better
use for my time, than to waste it in an idle conference like this."

" You say right," rejoined Geister, unmoved
by the peremptory tone of Peverell. " You
should have *much* to do, before you repair to
the grave of that rash fool whom you buried.
You see, my knowledge is not confined to what
has been. I am not ignorant of what is to be."

" I grant it," replied Peverell; " but were
you as well able to tell my thoughts, as you are

my movements, you could not shake my resolution to go on with this business."

" It was not for that I came," said Geister.
" I would have you see the end; and that you
may see it, I have presented myself before you."

" You tell me," retorted Peverell, " that you
come to save me. I ask you, from what or from
whom, and your answer is, from Fitz-Maurice;
but, in the same breath, you add, you are Fitz-
Maurice's deadly enemy, and that it is your hatred of him, not your love for me, which insti-
gates you. It follows, therefore, that your first
and great object is, to injure him in some way
or other; while, whatever of benefit may result
to me, can only be the contingent result of that
mischief you meditate towards him. Again, I
say, I put back the boon, proffered upon those
conditions."

" I make no conditions," replied Geister,
coolly. " I am here to offer you a service, in a
plain, direct way. It is yourself that extracts
conditions out of the intended service, by a subtle

logic which, I confess, goes quite beyond my simple apprehension."

" Well, then," said Peverell, " if that be the case, shew me at once the service you aim at, and I at once will tell you whether it pleases me to accept it ?"

" Why, that's honestly said !" exclaimed Geister. " Now we come to it, without more tedious parley, like men who mean the thing they say ; and not as your wily statists do, whose nimble tongues, ever divorced from their hearts, outrun their own thoughts to catch the thoughts of others. Well, then, to the matter : Go not to the Abbey to-night—no, nor to the church-yard."

" Why ?" inquired Peverell.

" Look you, now, how unreasonable you are !" rejoined Geister. " You would exact full confidence ; and yet will render none. Tell me you will be at home, when the clock strikes eleven ; and I promise to be with you at that same hour, to tell you why I bid you keep the house."

" How does this agree with your assurance, not five minutes since, that you came not to shake my resolution, but would have me see the end of this business ?" replied Peverell.

" There are enow for to-night," said Geister, " without you ; and the *end* is *not* to-night."

" This cannot be !" answered Peverell, after a moment's pause. " I must have other and stronger grounds, to abjure my oath of honour, and deny my own eager spirit the satisfaction it hungers for, than a vague premonition ; with a loose promise from one whom I know not, that, at the very hour when the course I am advised to will be irrevocable, if I adopt it, I shall be instructed why it was prudent in me to do so. Either disclose all now, and let me freely judge before-hand ; or leave me in the undisturbed possession of the motives I already have, for what I mean to perform."

" I should have thought," replied Geister, in

a taunting tone, " that you had been sufficiently disciplined in obedience to mysterious mandates, and had long enough surrendered that free judgment you now stand for, to make the trial I would put you to no very severe exercise of your faith. *I* warn you of danger, and ask only some three or four hours to possess you of reasons which would justify my warning. Fitz-Maurice hath *given* you danger—hath put you all in jeopardy, and exacts unsatisfied obedience to the last. You, Marmaduke Peverell, who must have good and prevailing reasons, forsooth, to heed *me*, can shut your eyes, and, with no reason at all, cry, ' be it as thou sayst,' when *he* commands !"

" But—" said Peverell—

" But,—" interrupted Geister, reddening with anger, " but it jumps with your humour —it flatters your vanity—it cajoles your pride —to be a seeming instrument of discovering wonders—to walk the street, and be pointed at by the finger of the multitude as the

fearless he who nightly plays with horrors
—to be the silly moth, which flutters round
the gaudy flame that first singes, and at last
consumes it! I am a stranger! You know
me not! and, therefore, it would derogate from
your new born independence of mind, to exe-
cute my unexplained injunctions. Did you
know this Fitz-Maurice, better than you know
me, when first he came and worked upon your
then easy nature? Do you know him now?
Can you tell we whence he came?—whither he
goes?—or why he hath stirred you and others
to abide the issue of this damned enterprise?
No! The innocent lamb that is led to slaughter,
could as easily bleat out a reason why it sub-
mits its throat to the butcher's knife, as you
assign a valid cause for what you do."

"Why this sudden wrath—this bitter rail-
ing?" said Peverell.

"Because it makes me mad," replied Geister,
with increased warmth, "to see an honest nature like yours, betrayed to its inevitable undo-

ing, by the treachery of those noble qualities which should be its bulwark and salvation."

" You armed me against yourself," answered Peverell, " when you told me you were the enemy of Fitz-Maurice, and came to me to make me a weapon in your hands for his destruction."

" I *am* his enemy !" exclaimed Geister, furiously—" but I would be your friend."

" Prove it," said Peverell, " by less suspicious evidence, and I will own myself your debtor."

" No !' answered Geister ; " fail my vengeance, rather, and perish you !"

" Amen ! with all my heart !" added Peverell. " I know not the mischance which could spring from this business, and find me unprepared."

" You are immoveable, then ?" said Geister.

" Aye, as the rock," answered Peverell.

" You will not be fore-warned," continued Geister.

" I will not be the idle straw, that is lifted from the earth, and driven to and fro by every gust that blows from heaven," replied Peverell.

" We shall meet again," said Geister, rising; " and when we do, I prophesy you will ask, with tears, what now you spurn with scorn."

" And then," answered Peverell, proudly, " you may refuse, with scorn, whate'er it is I shall implore with tears."

" No! thou stubborn fool! ASK EVEN AT THE TWELFTH HOUR, and Conrad Geister will not deny thee !"

With these words he quitted the room ; and before Peverell had well recovered from the amazement and irritation which his visit had excited, he was called upon to give audience to the mayor, who had come in a great flurry to confer with him.

" Who was that travelled gallant I met at the door ?" said his worship, as soon as he was seated. " But never mind—I have much weightier matters to talk about. Master Peverell," he continued, leaning on his elbow, and supporting his head with the fore finger of his right hand, while his countenance assumed an expression of infinite gravity—" Master Peverell, there must be no more of these devilries— there must be an end put to these vagaries of Beelzebub—I must interpose my authority to stop these sacrilegious junketings—or I shall not be able to answer for myself, as becomes myself, before the council."

" What does your worship mean ?" said Peverell.

" I mean," answered the mayor, " that I have done wrong—very wrong; I see it—I am sensible of it—and I sorely condemn myself. I have aided and abetted in the carrying on of this ugly business, when I ought to have forbidden it by virtue of my authority. The people begin to cry out upon me—and not upon me only, but upon the state itself, one of whose humblest, though most loyal officers, I profess myself to be. I am in danger of a *premunire*, Master Peverell."

" I hope not," replied Peverell, with be-coming solemnity.

" I hope not, too," added his worship, " but my fears are stronger than my hopes, I can tell you. For how can I purge myself of all wilful connivance, when it shall be thrown into my teeth that I have provided you with meat and drink, with wine and food—good wine, and delicate viands, as you must allow—the very ammunition, as it were, with which to carry on this unholy work !"

" But why unholy, your worship—why un-holy ?" interrupted Peverell.

" Tut ! tut !" interrupted the mayor : " question me no reasons, when you have facts as plenty as midges after rain on a summer's evening. Where is Wilfrid Overbury ? Tell me that an' you can ; and if you cannot, give me no quips and quirks about mere words. I say, the matter must be differently inquired into. The archbishops and the bishops must be made acquainted with it—it must become an affair of the ecclesiastical court, that men's minds may be quieted. You know not, perchance, but it is time you did, that I cannot answer for the public peace, if peace be not speedily restored within the Abbey—but of this anon. What mainly concerns my present visit to you, is touching this said Wilfrid Overbury. Strange rumours are abroad, and men's tongues begin to wag saucily upon the subject. Can you inform me where he is, or what has become of him ?"

" In truth I cannot," replied Peverell, " though I could certainly give a shrewd guess upon the subject. But of what kind are the rumours you speak of ?"

" Marry, that he is no where to be found," answered his worship.

" Humph !" said Peverell, musing ; " that is such a rumour as men might circulate who should hint, with a grave shake of the head, that the perfumed violet grows on no sunny bank at Hallowe'en."

"Moreover," continued his worship, "it is whispered that you know something about his disappearance."

"There, again," replied Peverell, still musing, "supposition treads upon the heels of probability. No man more likely than myself to know something of the matter."

"Further," added his worship, "they talk of a fray that fell out between you and Overbury yesterday morning, wherein he wounded you."

"Even so," rejoined Peverell; "you see I still carry my arm in a sling."

"And lastly," said his worship, "which brings me to the point at once, some adder-tongued Jacks there be, who do not scruple to shrug their shoulders, and with a mysterious knitting of their brows, drop slanderous phrases about *secret revenge, dark doings,* and *midnight opportunities !*"

" How !" exclaimed Peverell.

" It is what I have heard," replied his worship ; " and in the equal exercise of official
duty and private friendship, I held it meet to
come and tell you."

" The scald knaves !" said Peverell. " Do
they think me a night stabber, or that I have
cut his throat, upon advantage, when I might
have ta'en his life in open day, as the lawful
forfeit of his attempt upon my own ?"

" They do not absolutely stretch their speech
to such a license," replied his worship, " but
they go near to do it."

" While I feel indignant," answered Peverell, " at this foul suspicion, I cannot but acknowledge there is cause for the busy voice of
rumour. With regard to what hath befallen
Overbury, I am as free from taint in all that
concerns it, as in what hath befallen Wilkins,
Vehan, or my friend—my best friend—Hugh
Clayton."

Peverell then procceded to relate all the

circumstances that led to Overbury's fate, as well as the manner of its taking place. He also mentioned the intention of himself and the rest, to visit the Abbey again that night, together with the hour, the place of meeting, and the probability that, whatever the mystery might be which was involved in the events that had hitherto occurred, it was on the eve of being cleared up. His worship listened with manifest wonder to Peverell's statement; and when he had concluded, shook his head, with the grave solicitude and self-complacency of a man, who not only had others to take care of, but who saw infinitely further than his neighbours into a difficulty.

"It is just what I expected!" said he; "just what I expected—but I have nothing here," he continued, pointing to his forehead—"no more brains than a woodcock, if there be an end, till I have imparted certain things which I wot of, to the Council, and till the bishops take it in hand. Mark you that, Master

Peverell ! I expect a messenger from the court
to-morrow. If he come not, so; but if he
come not, *certes* I go next day to London, and
then you shall see what ought to have been
done from the first. It is fit, however, I should
act as becomes mine office. Therefore I say,
leave the matter where it is : go no more, but
wait till I have seen the Council. An' you
will not do so, be answerable yourselves for all
that follows. And so I take my leave, washing
my hands of the business altogether."

His worship departed ; and Peverell had leisure to reflect a little, not only upon what he
had just heard, but upon his singular interview
with Conrad Geister. With respect to the latter,
his reflections ended in nothing, for he could not
form even the shadow of a reasonable conjecture
as to who he was, or what could have been the
specific object of his visit. He determined, however, to mention it to Fitz-Maurice, should he
find an opportunity. With regard to Overbury,
he was only surprised it had not previously

occurred to him that the removal of his body was a circumstance which must inevitably give rise to various suppositions. He wondered, indeed, that neither he nor any of the others had questioned Fitz-Maurice upon the subject, if it were only that they might have a plausible explanation to give ; for though Overbury had no family, he kept two domestics in his house, who would naturally raise an inquiry, when they found their master did not return home. This they had done ; and hence, as the day advanced, the growing rumours which had diffused themselves from mouth to mouth, some of them, as it seemed, involving himself.

CHAPTER X.

THE night came! The eleventh hour approached, and consternation filled every mind !
The people ran to and fro, or collected in terrified groups, to gaze upon the appalling scene
that presented itself ! The Abbey again appeared like one huge mass of 'glowing fire ; again
were beheld careering flames, which sometimes
shot along the walls, as if they were burning
spears and arrows ; at others, slowly unfolded
themselves into unknown shapes ; and then, curled up the grey towers, which seemed to melt in
their fierce embrace. The earth shook beneath :

the roof heaved and rolled above ; the walls reeled ! In the lurid air were seen grisly forms and dusky shadows flitting about, or slowly sailing round and round with enormous wings, which made a momentary darkness as they passed along. The wind roared ; and, ever and anon, amid its gusty pauses, were heard screaming and howling in the sky, which mingled fearfully with the groans and cries of affrighted men, women, and children, who ran wildly about the streets. Every house cast forth its tenants. The sick, the lame, and the aged, rushed out to cling for protection to husbands—fathers—sons—who had joined the frantic multitude. But no one talked of comfort : no one breathed the word of consolation. The boldest, stood calmly waiting for the worst ; the weakest, and the most timid, already found that worst in their fears, and wept and shrieked for aid.

One alone, in that night of horror, looked on and smiled. It was Fitz-Maurice !

As if no earthly passion found a place within

his bosom—as if no human impulse throbbed within his heart—as if, with man's form only, he owned the unshrinking spirit of some god or devil, he surveyed, unmoved, the terrific scene. The bell tolled the hour of eleven, and the ground rung beneath the furious tread of his courser's feet.

De Clare, Peverell, Mortimer, Lacy, Hoskyns, Walwyn, and Owen Rees, were already assembled by the obscure grave of Kit Barnes. Fitz-Maurice came. He alighted not—he spoke not—but on his features sat an expression of serene joy. He beckoned them forth from the churchyard, and they slowly gathered round him in silence. Mephosto looked at them with malignant exultation, as he drew back his steed to make room for them near Fitz-Maurice. They were alone. None knew of their purpose to be there, and they had reached the gloomy spot unobserved. At intervals they heard, floating on the breeze, the discordant voices of the distant multitude—the sudden cry—the loud

shout—the growing murmur, confusedly mingled with the howling of the wind, and with the
unearthly noises, like dismal wailings, or the
moanings of deep anguish, which issued from
the Abbey.

" Methinks," said De Clare, drawing his
cloak round him, and folding his arms, while
he addressed Fitz-Maurice, " methinks you
were well advised when you said, last night, we
stood close upon the unveiling of these mysteries."

" I was prepared for this," replied Fitz-
Maurice, " and more than this."

" More !" exclaimed Walwyn.

" Aye, more !" responded Fitz-Maurice;
" else why did I forewarn you ? Why hem you
round with a solemn oath, to guard against one
faltering step from a timid spirit, in the final
act ? But we have not met to talk. Follow
me !"

" One word," said Peverell, laying his hand

upon the neck of Fitz-Maurice's charger. " Do
you know Conrad Geister ?"

" What of him ?" replied Fitz-Maurice.

" Do you know him ?" repeated Peverell.

" I do *not* know Conrad Geister," answered
Fitz-Maurice. " Why do you ask ?"

"He is your sworn enemy," replied Peverell—
" one who spoke of what you were in the mountains and vallies of Scandinavia—one who
sought me this evening in my house, and wasted
an hour, or thereabouts, in earnest persuasion,
to keep me from coming here."

Mephosto galled his steed with the rein, to
make him curvet and plunge towards where
Peverell stood.

" For this it was," exclaimed Fitz-Maurice,
looking at Mephosto, "that you charmed me into
sleep, and left me! You shall groan for it, filthy
thing, ere long." Then, turning to Peverell, he
added, "If you remember the words of my letter,
you will understand why I honour your noble
firmness ; and why he that *hath* faith shall *have*

it ! But now you are answered—and now let us forward."

Fitz-Maurice moved slowly in the direction of the Abbey ; Mephosto followed close behind ; the others walked by his side. When the people saw them, they uttered a loud cry, and fled. They could see only the gigantic figure of Fitz-Maurice ; his sable ostrich plume waving in the wind ; his long black mantle streaming behind ; his courser proudly pawing the earth, as he advanced ; and Mephosto's hideous form in the rear. They knew not what it was, and they were dismayed.

As they approached the Abbey, the noises were redoubled. Monstrous shadows reared themselves in threatening attitudes along the walls—the bell tolled, and its beat was like the roaring of cannon—purple and sulphureous flames seemed to burst from the windows— the earth trembled beneath their feet—the rushing winds blew from every quarter of the heavens : —blazing meteors flashed across the darkened sky—fiery hail fell before them at each step, as if to drive them back—corpse-like faces grinned and chattered around them—unseen, icy hands clasped theirs—night ravens shrieked : toads croaked, and adders hissed : the ground was strewed with loathsome reptiles of all kinds : low, mourning voices smote their ears, crying, " Beware ! beware !" and a fast swelling river of blood, seemed to exhale from the earth, like a moat, before the doors of the Abbey !

Within the portal itself stood the Old Man, even as he shewed himself on the night when Kit Barnes entered. In his right hand, the arm of which was bared up to the shoulder, he held the crucifix aloft, as then he did ; but instead of flames of fire issuing from it, when he waved it furiously over his head, there appeared the sacred image of the Redeemer, in meek and patient suffering !

At sight of this, Fitz-Maurice stopped ; and elevating his voice above the horrid tumult, exclaimed,—" Behold yon symbol ! By its

holy power I conjure ye, be men! May the
sacred spirit of the host of martyrs inspire you,
and animate your hearts! Forward!—and remember! he who looks behind, makes himself
a traitor to the cause he has espoused!"

So saying, he again gave his steed the rein.
But at that instant, all was darkness and death-
like silence without! Nothing was visible, save
the grey stone walls of the fabric, and gleaming lights, that flashed in fitful radiance through
the windows; nothing was audible but a faint
stifled cry of woe within! Arrived at the
door, Fitz-Maurice sprung from the saddle,
and giving his courser to Mephosto, exclaimed,
" Tarry for the hour! If I come not, then
come not thou, till I bid!"

" I *will* tarry," croaked Mephosto; " or.
at thy mighty bidding, come!"

Fitz-Maurice threw open the doors of the
Abbey, and entered, followed by Peverell,
Lacy, De Clare, Walwyn, Mortimer, Hoskyns,
and Owen Rees. A loud yell, as if proceeding

from a thousand iron voices, smote their ears; and then, a horrid laughing burst forth, which seemed to come from above, below, and around them. This was followed by dismal shrieks, which grew fainter and fainter, till at last they subsided into what seemed a funereal dirge, accompanied by the swelling tones of an organ! As these died away, a solemn stillness prevailed.

The interior was lighted, if light it could be called, with that kind of dusky gloom which is shed over every object by the descending shadows of evening. The eye could distinguish neither the height, nor the length, nor the breadth of the aisles. But pale phantoms, in shrouds and winding sheets, and in every stage almost of mortal decay, were visible. Some looked, as if life had just departed—others with that green and yellow hue, as if they had not lain in the earth a week—some shewed incipient rottenness, in the loss of lips, and eyes, and cheeks—others, with the features dissolving into putrid liquefaction—some were brushing away the worms that crawled out of their ears and mouth—and some, more horrible still, seemed to dress up their dry, fleshless bones, in the living characters of thought and passion! On every side, these hideous spectres were seen, sweeping slowly along in the air, or gliding upon the ground, or stalking backwards and forwards, with noiseless motion. Sometimes they would bring their pestiferous faces close ; and their smell was of corruption ; but if the up-lifted hand was raised to put them back, it passed through mere vacancy !

At the very entrance, almost, stood the Old Man, with the crucifix held above his head, and glaring like a demon at Fitz-Maurice, while rage, defiance, and scorn successively dwelt upon his features. His head and feet were bare ; his right arm naked to the shoulder ; and round his body, an ample purple vest or robe, confined by a crimson girdle, with a curiously wrought clasp of gold, which fastened beneath the bosom, and flickered to the eye, like gently undulating flame. He did not utter a word ; but remained motionless, as if it was his intent to dispute the further progress of Fitz-Maurice, who also paused for a moment.

As to the feelings of those who were following him, it were vain to attempt, by any description, to convey a notion of their intensity. Peverell, De Clare, and Lacy were the only ones of whom it could truly be affirmed they *felt* no fear : the first, from native intrepidity of character—the second from disdain—and the third from habit. Of the other four, it could only be said they *expressed* none. Walwyn thought of his kinsman's death, and hardly cared how soon he followed him. Mortimer played with his lovelock, and breathed short. The Welchman kept his hand upon the hilt of his sword, and raising himself upon his toes, essayed to peep over the shoulders of the others, at what might be coming. Hungerford Hoskyns touched him on the elbow, and in a whisper, that partook of something between a groan and a laugh, exclaimed, " I think we are cracking the shell of this business now—keep close, for the love of God !"

Fitz-Maurice, calm and undaunted, advanced. The Old Man receded a few paces, but still confronting his adversary. The grim shadows flit about in quicker motion, and become more ghastly. Fitz-Maurice continues to walk slowly onwards, and the Old Man gives way, step by step. The ground rocks and heaves, and the stones cleaving asunder, a deep, dark grave yawns before them ! The Old Man points to it with an air of deriding malignity. Fitz-Maurice bows his head in silence, as he still proceeds. They have all passed the grave. Suddenly, a dismal howl, a long, deep, and melancholy moan, break upon the stillness of the scene.

Again the ground rocks and heaves—again the pavement opens, and another grave gapes beneath their feet ! The Old Man points to it, as before. Fitz-Maurice raises his eyes to heaven, and his lips move, as if in prayer. A louder howl, a longer and a deeper moan, are heard; but Fitz-Maurice advances, upon the still retreating footsteps of the Old Man, whose looks betray rage and amazement!

And now, upon the leaden-coloured mist that had hitherto enveloped them, there grew a streaming brightness of saffron-tinted light, which emitted a most noisome odour, and filled the whole surrounding space; but it was too opaque to render visible more than a small portion of it. The Old Man plucked from his golden clasp a part of it, and cast it violently on the ground; when the earth opened with a tremendous noise, and from the rugged chasm ascended sulphureous flames of roaring fire! The blue glare fell upon their faces as they passed, and gave a frightful expression to the convulsed features of the Old Man, who found himself unable to arrest their progress.

He starts—stops—thrusts the cross into his bosom—draws thence a broad sable fillet, inscribed with mystic characters, in silver, which he binds round his head—throws himself upon the ground, and lies motionless for nearly a minute. Fitz-Maurice unsheathes his sword, and springs towards him; but at the moment when his arm is raised to strike, the blade shivers into a thousand pieces like so much brittle glass, and the Old Man rising, looks at him with a scoffing air, while he points exultingly, to two more graves which are seen slowly opening before him! As they gradually widen themselves, there appears, in one, the spectre of Kit Barnes, with outstretched arms, gaunt, grim, and terrible! In the other, a dark-red fluid, which gives it the semblance of a cistern of blood!

The Old Man stands between them, and by his gestures defies Fitz-Maurice to advance! The defiance avails him nothing. Fitz-Maurice, answering the silent challenge of his adversary only by a placid smile, does advance; and the Old Man springing back several feet, with a loud scream, tears the fillet from his

head.   He breathes upon it thrice; then holds
it out, and as it melts away, dropping like
liquid diamonds on the ground, he utters
words of uncouth sound, and trembles violently !

And now, the saffron tinted light which had
diffused itself, disappeared; and a thick vapour
succeeded, which went on deepening and deepening, till there was total darkness! The eye
could distinguish no object, save the grisly
phantom shapes, which glided about more
brightly horrible through the surrounding
gloom. A profound stillness prevailed; no
one spoke—no one moved. At length, there
appeared along the walls on each side, and at
each end, black dimly burning tapers, held by
skeleton hands. These, as they slowly multiplied, shed a sombre, funereal light upon the
whole interior of the abbey; and the likeness
of a marble tomb of massy structure and
vast dimensions was visible! The doors were
closed; but beside them stood two spectral

figures, each with a glittering key, as of burnished gold, in its hand. The portals were surmounted with a white alabaster tablet, upon which appeared the name of BENJAMIN LACY! A few paces behind, was the Old Man, surveying with an air of seeming triumph, the wondrous scene around him.

Fitz-Maurice, too, surveyed it with an anxious look. For a moment, he appeared irresolute and disconcerted, while exulting mockery sat scoffing on the Old Man's brow. The bell strikes the first hour of twelve! The presence of a mightier power is confessed, in the writhings and contortions of the Old Man—in the rocking of the walls—in the trembling of the earth—and in the groans that burst from beneath the earth!

Fitz-Maurice advances—he is followed by Peverell—by Lacy! The iron portals of the tomb fly open! Within, reclining on a bier, appears the pale, shrouded form of Lacy's wife—the sainted mother of his Helen! She points to a vacant place by her side, and a solemn voice issues from the sepulchre, crying, " COME !" Lacy staggers towards the tomb, but the Old Man rushes forward—seizes him, and holds him back ! A death-like silence reigns.

The chimes have ceased—the twelfth hour has tolled. A loud knock is given at the Abbey door, and the words " HUSBAND COME !— THE CROSS IS MINE !" in tones of silvery sweetness, are heard without. Another knock, and again that gentle invocation ! A third—and a third time it is pronounced !—The doors roll back their ponderous bulk, and Helen Lacy enters !

" Behold !" exclaimed Fitz-Maurice.

Peverell and Lacy look, and they see the figure of Helen, attired like a bride, in virgin white, and veiled, advancing slowly along. They see ONLY her ! But before their tongues can exclaim—" Where is De Clare ? — where Walwyn ? — where Mortimer ? — where Hoskyns ? — where Owen Rees ?" their unasked questions are fearfully answered. Each grave they had passed is tenanted! And as the shuddering Helen walks towards the altar, each grave heaves to its surface, at her approach, the lifeless and disfigured form of its fresh inhabitant!

Horror and consternation possess the minds of Lacy and Peverell. The latter thinks of all that Conrad Geister said; the former, of all that had fallen from his daughter's lips. He half doubts, half believes, it is she who silently and slowly paces along. He knows not her dress; and her veil conceals her features. He is still in the grasp of the Old Man, at the entrance of the tomb; but his whole and undivided attention is elsewhere. His heart beats high—his mouth is parched—his straining eyes follow the movements of Helen!

Fitz-Maurice, too, gazes upon her! Hope and despair alternately sustain and smite his agitated soul. The Old Man foams with agony and rage, the blackened froth gathering on his lips, as he glares at the spotless maiden, in whose purity of purpose he reads his own damnation! Peverell has his hand upon the arm of Fitz-Maurice, who, with a stern look, imposes silence upon his intrepid follower.

Helen remembered well, and performed nobly, the task enjoined her. She spoke not— she uttered no exclamation—though affrighted almost beyond mortal bearing, by what she saw. With a majestic step, and a lofty air, as if she felt the eye of Heaven were upon her, she advanced towards the altar; and when she stood beneath it, she cast back her veil. Then, for the first time, she saw her father! and a smothered shriek died within her lips, as she beheld the angelic vision of her mother in the tomb beyond! Then, too, Lacy recognised his daughter, and consoling doubts yielded to paternal anguish.

Helen looked at him with radiant eyes: with an ecstatic expression of bliss upon her features, which proclaimed the kindling consciousness of her heart, that she had done well in all she had done, and that now was to be the glad reward of all, in delivering him from his jeopardy. " Oh that I might speak !" was her silent ejaculation; " and abridge, but by a single moment, the wretchedness that clings to thy noble spirit." She caught one glimpse, too, of the dark, penetrating eye of Fitz-Maurice, and read its language with a proud smile.

She took off the SIGNET; placed it on the altar; knelt—and with such fervid devotion as expiring saints might feel, while the yet struggling soul is preparing for its flight to realms of everlasting bliss, already opening in bright glory to its view, she prayed : " *Forgive me ! I know not what I do : but thy will be mine !*" Choral voices catch her words, and hymning strains are heard above, chaunting in solemn response, " FORGIVE ! FORGIVE !"

She rises—places the signet again upon her finger, and lifts her hand to Heaven, as she looks towards her father. At that moment Lacy speaks.

" Helen ! cursed be the arts by which you work ! See me perish, and abjure them !"

" See him perish, OR abjure them !" screamed forth the Old Man.

" I implore you !" added her father ; " be-gone, and let thy trust be in God alone !"

Helen paused : her arm was still extended— her bosom heaved convulsively—her brain whirled—her knees smote each other—her countenance was awfully sublime—her eyes were fixed in the up-raised expression of intense piety. Fitz-Maurice rushed towards her— knelt, and in the wildest agony of speech ex-claimed, " You deny me, then !" These words—that voice—that attitude—that myste-rious being, subdued all fear and hesitation. The next moment, " I COMMAND THEE—OBEY !" fell from her lips !

The Old Man, with a loud and terrific yell, quitted his grasp of Lacy, and the two spectral figures which had guarded the doors of the tomb, thrust him in. They close. The Old Man darts to where Helen stands, takes the Cross from his bosom, and lays it on the altar. Instantly the lights vanish, and there is total darkness again! Fires flash around—the blue lightning, in forked wrath, darts through the windows—the volleying thunder bursts, and rebellows, till the deep foundations of the Abbey seem to shake to their bottom—and the fierce wind-storm raves round the walls, like the discordant howlings of the spirits of the abyss!

CHAPTER XI.

BY degrees the deafening tumult subsided, and at last, not a murmur was heard within or without the Abbey. Then it was that Peverell, who had stood motionless all the time, his senses nearly overpowered, perceived above him a small circle of exceeding brightness, from which gradually proceeded a beam of light—at first, no larger than the stem of an olive branch, but, as it descended, expanding itself, till it spread into a flood of soft yellow radiance over the altar.

By its lustre, which completely illumined

more than half of the interior, while the whole
was rendered partially visible, he saw that himself, Fitz-Maurice, and Helen, were the only
living creatures within the walls. All else had
disappeared! All that had appalled their eyes
had vanished! Where graves had yawned, the
smooth pavement spread itself, as if cemented
by the lapse of ages. Where the visionary
tomb had stretched its cold arms for the gallant veteran, was now unencumbered space;
and the murky air, that had so lately been
peopled with hideous phantoms, was now suf-
fused with the streaming effulgence of that
light by which he was enabled to note these
changes.

He looked towards the altar. On its topmost
step stood Helen, in the same attitude, with
extended arm, one foot advanced, and her head
thrown back, as when she pronounced the spell-
compelling words. Her eye still bent its gaze
upon the spot where she had seen her father;
but it was glazed and rayless—the blood had

left her cheeks; her half unclosed lips were pale and moved not. The horror of that moment which had thus petrified her, sat grimly visible on every feature; and she appeared only a marble image of that being which was once Helen Lacy. Peverell doubted whether life still lingered in her veins.

At the foot of the steps knelt Fitz-Maurice, in devout, but silent prayer. His hands were clasped, his eyes raised towards the altar, and his countenance, upon which fell the full radiance of the descending light, beaming with holy ecstacy. He seemed absorbed in the vehemence and magnitude of his own feelings. There was an inexpressible degree of dignity and grandeur in his appearance, arising not less from his gigantic stature, his costly sable vestments, his towering ostrich plume, and ample velvet mantle, than from the glow of exalted piety, which spread over his fine and intensely animated features.

Peverell contemplated these two with a mind

wholly incapable of reflecting upon what had taken place. His mental faculties were stunned. He knew certain things had happened; but beyond that mere naked assurance of a fact, of which his outward senses of sight and hearing had informed him, he knew nothing. The very loneliness and silence of his present situation appalled him. The world, beyond those walls, was a cypher, a blank, to his imagination at that moment; and within them, Helen presented herself as a breathing statue only, (if indeed, she did breathe,)— while Fitz-Maurice, who at no time appeared to be touched with human sympathies, now, less than ever, seemed clothed with mortal attributes.

He felt he was ALONE; and the sense of desolation which accompanied that feeling, was in no degree mitigated by the reflection that he lived. Nay, in the chaotic tumult of his thoughts, he almost questioned his own identity —he doubted, almost, whether what he now saw was reality, or whether it was not a part of that astounding mystery whose terrific illusions had passed before him. His eye involuntarily glanced round the Abbey, in search of Mortimer, De Clare, Walwyn, and those other friends who had entered it with him ; and he shuddered as his perturbed mind whispered to his heart, " They are gone !"

He was roused from these clouded meditations by a piercing shriek which burst from Helen ; as if at that moment, a sudden consciousness of her situation had broken in upon her in all its overwhelming horrors. She buried her face in her hands, and sunk gently down upon the steps of the altar. Fitz-Maurice sprung from his attitude of devotion, and raising her up, bore her to a seat, before Peverell had power to move or speak. With a reeling step, and still glancing wildly behind, or from side to side, he approached her ; she looked both at him and Fitz-Maurice ; but there was evidently no recognition of either.

As Fitz-Maurice bent over her, his long

black plume drooped before her. She played
with the feathers and smiled, and played and
smiled, as a laughing infant would in its nurse's
arms. He put them back ; and then she sighed,
as if it grieved her to be denied so innocent a
pleasure. She spoke not a word. Fitz-Maurice raised her hand to his lips, kissed it, and
exclaimed, "Peerless maiden! what a price
hast thou paid down for my ransom!"

She started at the sound of his voice. Its
thrilling tones awakened a transient recollection of the past. She slowly lifted her eyes,
as though she dreaded to behold the being
from whom they had proceeded ; gazed at him
intently, for an instant, and then a vacant
laugh overspread her face. But her eye glanced
upon the signet, and hastily withdrawing her
hand from Fitz-Maurice, who still held it, she
exclaimed, with seeming anger and shame,
"Fye upon you! you are naught—I am married now! should my lord know of this, how

might he take it of me?" She then laid her hand in her lap, and continued wistfully to gaze at it.

Peverell beheld this scene, not only without emotion, but without once recollecting that the signet which had worked such fatal consequences, was the same which Helen had so mysteriously demanded of him. Fitz-Maurice, who perceived his distraction, led him away from where Helen sat, lost in the stupor of her own griefs, and thus addressed him—

"Marmaduke Peverell! rouse thyself!—summon back thy scattered thoughts, and bend up thy great energies to the task that still awaits thee."

Peverell, like Helen, started at the sound of Fitz-Maurice's voice; but upon his spirits it acted like a stone dropped into a dull and stagnant pool, stirring the still waters, and quickening them with motion. His name pronounced by any living tongue, at that moment, would have produced the same effect. He awoke to himself, as if he had suddenly emerged from a long and oppressive dream.

"Rouse myself!" he exclaimed. "Why where are we? Where—"

"Aye," interrupted Fitz-Maurice, "where are *they?* It is that you would add."

"It is," replied Peverell.

"And you shall be answered," said Fitz-Maurice, sighing deeply, "when ALL is done."

"When ALL is done!" repeated Peverell. "Does there yet remain a thing to be accomplished?"

"There does," said Fitz-Maurice; "and it is you alone must do it."

"Must!" ejaculated Peverell.

"When I say *must*," rejoined Fitz-Maurice, "I would be understood to mean no more than this—that in the universal world there lives no being, save yourself, who CAN."

"What is it?"

"To know, and to perform," said Fitz-

Maurice, " have marked your resolute spirit throughout. Do you remember this?" he continued, drawing aside his hair, and pointing to the mark upon his forehead.

" I do," said Peverell. " It is the crimson trophy of your victory over the Magician of the den, when you were in Mauritania."

" So I called it," replied Fitz-Maurice, when first I sought you as a ' brave man ;' as one, ' who had that quality within you which makes daring a virtue, raising it above the mere display of sinews and quick passion:' as one who, ' when mine own adventure in Mauritania came o'er my mind, made me say in my heart, here is a man to do the like !' But, said I not likewise, when I called this the crimson trophy of my victory, ' there *are* times, indeed, when it seems to burn inwards to my brain : but I know how to quench its fires ?'"

" You did," answered Peverell.

" It burns inwards now !" exclaimed Fitz-

Maurice, pressing his hand violently upon his
brow. "It ever burns ! Sometimes with greater,
sometimes with less, scorching fierceness."

"And yet you know how to quench its
fires !" added Peverell.

"Even so !"

"Then why endure its pangs ?"

"Thou noble spirit !" exclaimed Fitz-Maurice, seizing Peverell's hand, "I owe thee
much—a vast, vast debt, which my poor
thanks can only confess, but never pay. It is
THOU must quench this fire ! Thou—and thou
alone."

"I !" ejaculated Peverell. "How ?"

"Do you see yon altar ?" he continued.

Peverell looked, and perceived what he had
not before observed, a long black curtain,
which descended from the lofty roof of the
Abbey, and entirely concealed the whole of the
altar, except the steps which led up to it.

"On that altar," said Fitz-Maurice, "lies
the Cross which was held in the hand of him

who disputed, step by step, our entrance here
this night.   The moment I possess that holy emblem, in the same moment, I am released from
this tormenting trophy.   But it is not my hand
that can take it thence.   It is not ANY hand
—but thine!"

"Methinks," said Peverell, "it were an easy
deed enough, to walk there straight and bring
it away. I'll do it! Yon streaming ray of
wondrous light will guide me, and while I could
talk about it, it shall be done."

"Be undaunted," replied Fitz-Maurice,
"and it will be done."

"Undaunted!" exclaimed Peverell, pausing,
as he was turning from Fitz-Maurice. "What
mean you?"

"You must be neither fore-warned nor fore-
armed," said Fitz-Maurice ; "but in the oath
you have taken, and in the promptings of your
own heart, find the motive for the act. I am
powerless here."

Peverell hesitated for a moment.   It was

only a moment. The next, placing his hand in Fitz-Maurice's, he exclaimed with a calm, resolute tone,

" By my oath, I swear, and by that which now swells within me—the Cross is thine, or I— am nothing !"

He had no sooner uttered these words than the light which had hitherto shed its lustre upon the altar, and dimly illumined the rest of the Abbey, vanished. He was in total darkness again. But while he was groping his way along, he felt the cool air fan his cheek ; and, looking up, could just descry the long black curtain slowly flapping backwards and forwards. Anon, it seemed to open in the centre, rolling back its heavy folds on each side ; and as it opened, a scene of horror grew more and more distinct to his sight.

The communion table appeared covered with a pall ; and on it was spread a splendid banquet ! Black tapers were burning, held, as before, by skeleton hands, and gave forth a red,

dusky flame. Seated round this table, he beheld his eleven friends—they who had all
perished—in the same habiliments as when
living! They spoke not—they moved not!
Their aspect was cold and stony! A death-like
silence prevailed! Behind each chair, stood
pale shadows, as if to wait upon the guests!

Excited, maddened, almost, as Peverell had
already been by the terrific visions of the night,
he felt himself hardly able to endure this fresh
trial of his resolution. His temples throbbed—
his heart palpitated—his bosom heaved with a
quicker and quicker respiration—his knees
smote each other—and his blood shot through
his veins like liquid flames! Silent and motionless, his aching eye-balls bent their gaze upon
this withering scene. All around him was so
awfully still! So unearthly! So hideous!
He looked behind. The gloom was too dense,
too impenetrable, to allow of his distinguishing
Fitz-Maurice, though he had as yet scarcely
moved half a dozen paces from him. He turned

his eyes towards where Helen sat; but the pitchy darkness shrouded her from his view. The tall black tapers threw no light beyond the table—not even sufficient to enable him to discern the steps of the altar. A cold and clammy sweat bedewed his limbs, and he felt an almost frantic inclination to dash himself upon the ground, and so, in desperation, shut out this chilling mockery of what had once been real.

He tried to convince himself that he was fooled by his own heated imagination; that it was a cheat, put upon him by his own eyes; and he drew nearer to the altar. But no! If he ever saw them living, he saw them now! It was impossible to deny that he beheld them.

There, sat De Clare, with his lip of scorn, and brow of bitter taunt. There, Wilkins, with his fair round face, cold blue eye, and dimpling cheek. There, the fantastic Mortimer, his mustachios newly trimmed, and his love-lock redolent of perfume. There, the gallant

Lacy, erect and martial in his veteran figure. There, the pensive, melancholy Vehan, e'en as he looked and sighed, and told of Alice Gray. There, the choleric Welchman, with up-turned nose, as if scenting out a quarrel. There, the swart Overbury, scowling like a tempest. There, the gay, good-natured Hungerford Hoskyns. There, the simple-hearted friend, the confiding, honest Clayton. There, the frank, courteous Walwyn. There, mine host, with merry, laughing eye and comely paunch, looking, as he was wont, proud of the goodly company around him. And there, too, the gaunt figure of the half fanatic, Kit Barnes!

At the top of the table was a vacant chair· At the bottom sat a figure veiled, or rather covered to the feet with a sable drapery, so that neither form nor feature was discernible.

Peverell draws nearer. His foot is on the first step. He pauses for a moment, and contemplates this spectral company. Is he awake? Or do they really bend their rayless eyes upon

him, and, with a sepulchral smile, invite him to
sit? His brain whirls—his sight grows dim!
Again he looks, and again they smile a ghastly
welcome! He cannot resist! He obeys! He
rushes up the steps, and takes his seat! He
hears a voice he has heard before, breathe in his
ear, " Welcome! Thou art the last!" He
doubts the evidence of his own senses. Clayton
sits beside him. He puts his hand upon his.
It has a more than icy coldness; and a shivering tremor runs through his veins. He looks
round the table. What stony eyes stare upon
him!—what marble lips mock at him! He
grows dizzy, and exclaims, " Why, then, I'll
mock the mockers!"

He rises—and in each cold hand places a
crystal cup, into which he pours sparkling wine.
He comes to the veiled figure, and he laughs
horribly as he places before it a goblet, mantling
to the edge. He returns to his seat, pours out
a flowing cup, and raises it to his lips—but
dashes it from him. It is filled with worms,

that crawl and cling to its golden brim! His
guests smile, and point to theirs. The worms
are heaving and rolling about! The pale shadows which stand behind, advance, and with
their fleshless hands remove the loathsome
vessels.

" This is brave fare!" exclaims the half
frantic Peverell. " Come! Eat!" He helps
each to costly and delicate viands, and then
himself. Toads and adders—lizards—beetles,
and spiders—creep, and crawl, and twine about
the table, instead of the dainty food he had
served. Peverell is covered with them. He
starts from his chair, and as he brushes them
off, addresses his spectral friends.

" Will you speak? You, De Clare,—where
are your biting taunts—your saucy gibes, and
your ready scoff? Mortimer! swear by your
manhood you will pledge me! Clayton! I am
thy friend—hast *thou* no word for me? Wilkins! thy bags are stored to bursting : lend me !
not on usance, but for the vanity of shewing

thou art rich. Vehan! breathe one sigh—or
let me see thee weep, or fold thy arms, and
dream of moonlight visions in the silent grove!
Wilfrid Overbury! master of the Scorpion!—
say thou'lt stab me, as thou didst thy innocent
child, an' I cross thee in thy savage humour,
when thou art desperate! What! nor eat, nor
drink, nor speak! Hence, grim shadows of
what you *were!*—hence, horrible visions! Hence!
Aye! – now you obey—now you move!—now
—Almighty God! How is this? Is it thus
you show me what you *are?*"

While he spoke, the seats on which they sat,
changed into the semblance of coffins! In each
was a corpse! Their vestments had fallen from
them; and they now stood round the table in
their grave clothes—yea, in their shrouds and
in their winding sheets!

The veiled figure still remained, and Peverell
seemed to see only it. There was something
even more terrible to his imagination in its silent
mystery, and hidden form, than in all the visible

horror by which he was surrounded. He knew not what it might portend, or for what it tarried. He arose : and it stood up at the same time ! He moved ; and it moved towards him !

" What art thou ?" he exclaimed.

" Ask even at the twelfth hour, and Conrad Geister will not deny thee," said a voice.

" What should I ask ?"

" To close thine eyes in sleep till sunrise," replied the voice.

Peverell slowly turned his head. The voice did not seem to issue from the veiled figure, but from lips that were near him. He looked, and there was no one !

He paused. His agitation was excessive. He felt that he could endure the conflict with himself no longer. All consciousness of where he was, and wherefore he had approached the altar, was fast departing from him. At that moment his eye fell upon the Cross, and he saw a halo, or faint roseate light, encircling the image of the Redeemer, which it still bore. It surrounded

it like a glory. A sudden recollection flashed
across his mind. The veiled figure is between
him and the Cross. He advances to take it. The
veiled figure advances too, and stands before him.

" What art thou ?" again exclaimed Peverell.

Its black drapery falls, and Peverell beholds
the pale likeness of DEATH ! The grim anatomy
brandishes his spear ; the coffined spectres gib-
ber, and their bones rattle—the attendant shadows glide about ! Peverell presses forward ;
the upraised spear is levelled ; Peverell hesitates,
and Fitz-Maurice is seen ascending the steps of
the altar. The bones drop with a hideous clattering from the phantom, and the Old Man appears ! His gleaming eyes are two flaming torches;
his hot breath, the blasts from a furnace ; his
livid face, the speaking agonies of a tortured
fiend ; and in his hand he grasped a shining sci-
mitar, which flickered like the nimble lightning
that shoots athwart the heavens, swift harbinger
of the gathering tempest.

" Slave of thy fate !" he roars, glaring fiercely

at Fitz-Maurice, and shaking the massive walls
of the Abbey with his voice; " Vassal of my
power !   What darest thou yet?   Avaunt !"

Fitz-Maurice points to the Cross, and in a solemn tone repeats the words of Peverell.   " By
my oath I swear, and by that which now swells
within me, the Cross is thine, or I—am nothing!"

Peverell hears the words.   With collected
strength, with all the energy of mind and body
that yet remains to him, he dashes forward—
seizes the Cross—and staggers towards Fitz-
Maurice, who snatches the holy symbol from his
hand, exclaiming, as he clutches it, " BY THIS I
TRIUMPH !—PERISH, UNCLEAN SPIRIT !"

A loud and dismal yell, and piercing shrieks
that might have awakened the dead, were all
that Peverell remembered after ; for, as he felt
the Cross pass from his relaxing grasp to the
eager gripe of Fitz-Maurice, his sight thickened,
his limbs refused their office, and he sunk to the
earth, exhausted by the sharp trials he had undergone.

CHAPTER XII.

WITH returning consciousness, came returning wonders. When Peverell unclosed his
eyes, he found himself still in the Abbey, but
alone. And he was seated at a table, round
which were ranged twelve empty chairs. The
table was exactly in the same place, spread
with the same kind of viands and wines, and
lighted with the same number of waxen tapers,
as when the mayor used to provide fit reception
for them, on those fearful nights, the remembrance of which now presented itself to his

mind, like the fragments of a half-forgotten dream. The taking of the cross—the voice of Fitz-Maurice, as he slowly ascended the steps of the altar, and repeated his own emphatic words—the veiled figure, with its appalling changes—the abhorred mockery of the banquet —the vision of his eleven friends, and all its portentous ghastliness – the form of Helen Lacy,— a babbling idiot, like a rich casket, robbed of its master gem, but still rare and beautiful for its workmanship—the terrible array of unearthly power, that preceded her entrance,— all passed in dim and rapid succession before him. In vain he strove to disentangle his bewildered ideas; his mind was too feverish, too sensitive, to bear the retrospect. At every step, some hideous recollection started forth, in hues of such vivid reality, that the agony of remembering what had been, was surpassed only by the suffering of it.

He remained in this state of stupor for several minutes, languid alike, in body, and in mind, and rendered still more so, by the oppressive sense of that profound silence, and of that total solitude, which surrounded him. The thought that he *was* alone—the only living witness of miracles and events, whose mighty origin and unrevealed purpose, had eluded his grasp, like shadows—filled him with sadness. Why had it so chanced ? Or, if not the work of chance, why had it been so ordered? Why was he singled out, to float a little longer on the stream of life, that men might point at him, as the sole relic of a gallant bark, which had gone to pieces in the rough tempest of a strange, unfathomable mystery ?

While thus ruminating, he cast his eyes with a timid glance, round the Abbey ; when they were suddenly fixed in amazement upon an object which seemed the visible annunciation of his own secret and troubled thoughts. There appeared, stretching from side to side, the semblance of a broad belt of azure light, with edges, formed of thin, vapoury clouds,

whose swelling folds reflected a crimson glow,
like those of Heaven when tinged with the
first beams of the morning. Athwart this belt,
and occupying its whole extent, were these
words, traced in gigantic letters of vivid flame,
whose flickering brightness dazzled the sight:

"THOU ART THE LAST!"

Peverell gazed, but he uttered no exclamation. Still he gazed, and still the wondrous
scroll, terrible in its truth, shone with mysterious radiance before his eyes. It was as if the
incorporeal air had shaped itself into this silent
record of what he was: or, rather, as if
the whole invisible space bore the miserable
tidings; for wherever he turned his look—on
the right or on the left, above, or below, before or behind—there gleamed this azure belt,
with its words of lambent fire. It was every
where, yet never multiplied; always one and
the same; seeming to wait with nimble and
miraculous obedience upon each quick motion

of Peverell's eyes, as if created by that motion, rather than discovered by it only.

" I am, indeed, the last !" he exclaimed, with a grieved spirit, and covering his face with his mantle as he spoke.

There was something in the sound of even his own voice, thus giving utterance to his feelings of desolation, in the very place where that desolation had been produced, and where it then reigned in awful stillness around him, which weighed heavily upon his heart. But more heavily still was it oppressed, when he heard, in the low, stifled, tones of a funereal chaunt, or solemn requiem for the dead, these sad words, breathed with a mournful cadence from every part of the Abbey at once, and echoed back, in fainter and fainter notes, from the altar. While listening to the dirge-like strains, and subdued, even to tears, by their melancholy character, they gradually died away ; and then, there arose a voice of liquid sweetness and thrilling melody, such as might belong to what we deem of celestial minstrelsy, warbling in the air, to the responsive beat of fluttering wings. And this was its song of hope and gladness.

> Lonely mourner ! though the last,
> All thy trials now are past !
> Man of grief ! look up and see
> Silent friends who look on thee !
> Spell bound, but in spell so weak,
> That speak to each, and each shall speak.

Peverell raised his head—the mantle fell from his face—and he beheld, with emotions bordering upon frenzy, the table filled ! Yes ; once more he gazed upon Mortimer, upon De Clare, upon his friend Clayton, upon Lacy, Walwyn, and Vehan, upon the ferocious Overbury, upon Owen Rees, upon Hungerford Hoskyns, Wilkins, and mine host ! Each sat in the place he had been wont to occupy, and each bent his eyes upon the amazed Peverell, whose sight grew dizzy, and whose brain reeled with the memory of past horrors, which his staggering mind pictured to him as now about

to be acted over again. His first impulse was
to fly; but some secret power chained him to
the spot, and he felt himself as helpless as
infancy when he strove to move. Speak he
could not. His eyes glanced, with a wild and
hurried look, first upon one, and then upon
another; and still where'er they turned, they
met the fixed, silent gaze of all. Oh! that
fixed and silent gaze! That mute and earnest
look! It was horrible! Yet it was all that
partook of horror; for they had no longer the
stony glare, or the marble-like aspect, which
froze his blood before. There was motion in
their eyes, and life upon their cheeks; there
was the vital heaving of their manly bosoms;
and their lips had a ruby freshness of colour.
But they spoke not—they moved not; and all
else that proclaimed them mortal, wanting
these attributes of living man, only served to
shed a more appalling character over their
appearance. Why were they there, seeming
things of life, if, like shadows, they had nor

voice nor motion, to give the lie to fears that denied their seeming? At times, too, their eloquent eyes grew lustrous with thought, as though their minds laboured with intellectual conceptions, to which their tongues would fain give birth, but could not.

Next to Peverell was seated Clayton, the friend he had loved—the friend he still mourned. His hand rested on the table. With a dubious feeling, he gently placed his own upon it. It was warm !

" Gracious God !" he half exclaimed to himself, " how is this? I saw him dying: I saw him dead ! And now—Oh, it cannot be ! I am fooled to madness ! Or all that has been, has been a dream, and my waking senses are still struggling in the thrall of a night vision." Then, fixing his eyes upon Clayton, with a frightful expression, as dreading more the being undeceived, than the continuing in his delusion, he exclaimed, in a voice of forced .loudness, " If that thou livest, speak ! Here is my hand !

Take it, Hugh Clayton, if thou art what thou seemest!"

Peverell had no sooner uttered the words, than Clayton, turning towards him, observed,

" I profess myself no judge of metre, like your trained scholar; but I am marvellously well pleased with this ballad of Alice Gray !"

" God of Heaven !" exclaimed Peverell. " He speaks !"

Clayton, in his turn, looked with astonishment upon Peverell, and then round the table, as if to learn from the others the cause of that terror and amazement which sat upon the countenance of his friend. His eyes met those of Wilkyns.

" Lord preserve me !" he exclaimed, catching hold of Peverell's arm. " Do you see? As I am a Christian man, and a true Catholic, there sits poor Walter Wilkins who is dead !"

" Dead !" ejaculated Peverell. " Dead ! Who is dead? You—you ! No—no ! my dream is past. I have been sick, and dreamed

strange things.   But *you* are alive!   I see it—
I feel it—I hear it! and Walter Wilkins, too,
who looks upon me with that honest face—he
is alive, for lo! he wraps his cloak about him,
and now his lips unclose, to tell me I alone
have slept, and am awake."

Even as he said, it was.   At the pronouncing
of his name, by Peverell, Wilkins folded himself closely in his mantle, and spoke.   " By
the mass, gentlemen, I know not how you feel,
but I have not recovered yet from the freezing
darkness which followed that balmy roseate
atmosphere, of delicious fragrance.   Whew! I
verily think it hath congealed the marrow in
my back bone."

" Verily, I think the marrow in all my
bones is congealed," said Clayton in a whisper, to
Peverell.   " I wish he would go away again—
I don't covet speech with him, or—Lord God!
What is it shakes you so, Master Peverell,
and why do you look upon me so crazedly ?"

" Hush !" replied Peverell, and once more

he placed his hand on Clayton's, while with his eyes he scanned him from head to foot. Then he looked at Wilkins; then at the rest, whose fixed attitudes and silent gaze were still the same; and then, sinking into profound abstraction, he exclaimed, " Oh! this vile treachery of the senses! Whither will it lead me?" The next moment, as if he could no longer endure the maddening ambiguity, he started up, and wildly filling out a cup of wine, cried aloud, while raising it to his lips, " Vehan! De Clare! Mortimer! Walwyn! you, Hungerford Hoskyns — and you Owen Rees!— my throat is parched — my tongue cleaves to my mouth—rise, if thou canst, as I do, and ere I grow frantic,—pledge me!"

They all rose! And pouring out wine, they drank to Peverell, who with a convulsive laugh, dashed the goblet he held in his hand, to the ground, sunk into his chair, and exclaimed, in a voice almost suffocated with terror, " Shall the grave cast forth its dead, and shall the heart of him who beholds it, not tremble at the sight ?"

A different scene now ensued. Walwyn, when he saw his beloved kinsman, Vehan, standing before him, rushed forwards, and threw himself into his arms, mingling with his embraces, broken sentences of doubt, of joy, and of surprise; as his mind, in rapid succession, questioned whether he indeed lived, rejoiced in the belief that he did, and was bewildered by the miracle, if it were one. Vehan, who was wholly unconscious of the cause of this perturbation in Walwyn, gently disengaged himself, and fixed his eyes in silent astonishment upon Wilkins and Clayton, wondering at *their* presence; while De Clare, Mortimer, Owen Rees, Hoskyns, and Wal-wyn, looked not only upon them and Vehan, but upon Wilfrid Overbury and upon mine host, with equal amazement. Wilkins alone discovered nothing to move his wonder, ex-cept the wondering faces of those around him ;

and Clayton would have found himself in exactly the same situation, if Wilkins had been
away.

In the midst of these inexplicable mysteries
and disquieting recollections, and during some
brief conversation, which was carried on with
the most perplexing confusion of time, circumstances, and personal identity, the situation of
Peverell had entirely escaped their observation.
He sat, leaning back in his chair, with his arms
folded, his brow contracted, and his eyes wandering from one to the other, while his now calm
and pallid countenance indicated that he was surveying, with an untroubled spirit, a scene which
had ceased to distract, though it continued to
engross, his thoughts. He could no longer doubt
the reality of what he saw ; but confounded,
as he might well be, by the reality, still it was
far, far less appalling than that mockery of life,
that animated death, with which his disturbed
imagination had first clothed them.   There was
no comprehensible agency of this world that

could explain the mystery ; but his mind, having
subsided into that state of healthful action by
which he was enabled to recognise it as a mystery, and not as a phantasma, the violent agitation of his feelings gradually diminished.   He
heard them speak, and their voices fell upon his
ear, in tones that were familiar to it ; he beheld
them, and they looked and moved as he had ever
seen them look and move.   It was evident, however, that though his conviction of reality was
slowly strengthening itself, there still remained
upon his fancy a vivid impression of the fearful
images by which it had been haunted ; and the
inward struggle it produced was so visibly charactered in his countenance and manner, that
it attracted the greater notice, because strongly
contrasted with what had hitherto been his re-
markable firmness and equanimity.

"It surprises me not," remarked De Clare,
in reply to an observation of Walwyn: " for you
shall ever note, that those natures which, like
the pliant willow, bend to the gusts of fortune,

rear themselves again when the storm hath passed over ; but the stubborn oak, which defies the blast, and disdains to crouch, or triumphs o'er the tempest's fury, or falls a noble ruin, o'er-thrown by force greater than its own. We all have seen how this manly creature scorned the assaults which struck down feebler things ; but sure I am, that what this night hath chanced might well uproot even him !"

" By my manhood," rejoined Mortimer, " it was enough to uproot the Abbey itself, and bring it toppling about our ears. I protest, and blush not at the avowal, that at one time I would have given any part of my body, save my head, to know, of a certainty, that I should save all the rest."

" And you might have given your head," replied De Clare, " and been the richer by the gift ; for what we use not, is that we want not ; and what we want not, only stands in the way of something better which it would be profitable to have."

" As thou dost now," retorted Mortimer.

" Your proof, good Signior Lackwit," said
De Clare.

" It lies in the housewife's proverb," answered Mortimer. " The honey of the working
bee is better than the sting of the angry
wasp."

" Do you observe," interrupted Owen Rees,
" what enchantments, and necromancies, and
magics, and sorceries, still encompass us? If
I am not lunatic, mark you, there sits mine
host, and there, opposite him, the master of the
Scorpion—and there—

" The master of the Scorpion !" exclaimed
Clayton ; " by my troth, and thou art lunatic,
I ween ; for who among us knoweth of a master
of the Scorpion ?"

The Welshman looked at Clayton, and shook
his head. The rest, too, eyed him with so
strange a scrutiny, that Clayton began to ex-
amine himself, thinking there must needs be
some disorder in his apparel which attracted

their notice. But he discovered nothing ; and then he addressed Vehan, with an inquiry about Alice Gray, and what the men wanted with her. Vehan merely shrugged up his shoulders, while he ejaculated with a sigh, " Cross me thus in a church-yard, by the pale moon-light, and my spirit shall court thy discourse ; for it loves to mingle with the shadows of the tomb !"

" Did you hear that ?" observed Owen Rees, in a whisper to Hoskyns ; while Clayton, pointing to his head, remarked significantly to Walwyn, " I always thought it would come to this !"

" Yes," replied Hoskyns, in answer to the Welshman's question, " I did observe it ; and something better, I trow, than you observed me erewhile, when we entered the Abbey ; for though I implored you, for the love of God, to keep close to me, as we were cracking the shell of this business, the next moment you were gone."

" I !" said Rees.

"Aye, you ; and by my faith you must have been as fleet as the roc to get so nimbly to this well spread board."

" Now you mention it," quoth Owen, " I do remember me of such a speech ; but," he continued, with a look of growing astonishment, " an' I added thereto, that I remember me as truly how I found my way to this well-spread board you talk of, I should most villainously belie my memory, mark you."

" How ?" replied Hoskyns, " why——"

" Why," interrupted Peverell, in a solemn tone, who had noted the latter part of this conversation, " as a blind man treads an unknown path—by the guiding hand of another ! Before God ! I proclaim myself blind, even to utter darkness, in this mystery. My reason breaks down under the burthen imposed upon it, while my senses mock me with things at once impossible of belief, and of denial. What it is I mean, none of you can know ; for none of you have been my companions in all that I have witnessed ; yet there be some," (and he looked earnestly at De Clare, Mortimer, and those who had entered the Abbey with him that night,) " who *can* understand me ?"

" There be indeed, some of us," observed De Clare, " who read the same page as yourself in this strange volume ; who, like yourself, have silent thoughts for wonders, which the tongue can put into no form of words. But what is it you aim at when—"

" Peace, peace !" exclaimed Peverell. " For the love of God, touch not that string, if you would spare me torture and madness. There may be a time, hereafter, perchance, for such discourse ; and then we will confer like men, upon matters that could not now be talked of but as children prattle of their nurse's tales, with most devout belief and simple faith. For, look you there ! There sits one, whom, if I live myself, I saw, myself, stretched in death, most foully murdered : and there ano- ther, whom not mine own eyes only beheld

reel to the earth, in frantic agony at the reve-
lation of his crimes.   Yet, who shall say, they
are no longer of this world ?   Behold ! I but
breathe their names—my lips no sooner pronounce Wilfrid Overbury, and John Wintour,
than—aye ! e'en as you see—the life that is in
them starts into motion ! '

At that moment, Overbury, who had hitherto
sat in grim similitude of what he appeared on
the night when the phantom ship, and the
withering denunciation of Fitz-Maurice, blasted
his eyes and ears, suddenly sprung from his
chair, and with a wild and haggard countenance gazed round the Abbey, as if he expected still to see the visionary scene.   And
then he scowled, with a darker and fiercer
malignity than usual, upon those who were
about him, conscious that the lurking secret
of his heart had been dragged forth ; while
his very flesh seemed to quiver, as he caught
a glimpse of the persons of Vehan, Clayton,
and Wilkins.

As to mine host, it was easy to perceive he was sorely perplexed, listening to a sharp debate with himself, in which the probabilities of his own bed at The Rose being transformed into the Abbey, constituted the prominent topic; albeit there were certain recollections, too, whereof the kind-hearted Lacy was the principal object. For it so happened, that John Wintour had lain his head upon his pillow that night, with a firm determination to ride to Dunstable the next morning, and then and there to be either suddenly seized with a grievous sickness, or, in some other way, unexpectedly detained, till the term assigned by Fitz-Maurice for continuing their watchings, had elapsed. This said determination was what he now distinctly remembered : but finding himself in the Abbey, and *not* remembering how he came there, he very naturally began to conclude, that his intended journey to Dunstable was some dream he had had. Observing, however, Wilfrid Overbury seated opposite to

him, his perplexity was greatly increased ; for
he thought it impossible that his returning to
the Abbey with the keys, and calling upon him
to come forth, were also only dreams.

With a view to settle this point at once, he
gave a friendly nod to Overbury, and observed,
" I suppose you know that I came back to
look for you last night—I mean just now—that
is, before we *all* came back again, you know ;
after that poor gentleman, Master Philip
Vehan—the Lord preserve me ! there he is !
and, as I have a soul to be saved, Master Clayton, and Master Wilkins too !—I crave your
pardon—it couldn't be I who came back,
because I was in bed, and went to Dunstable,
and did not return till it was all over. Oh,
Lord ! what's the matter with me? I am not
in the Abbey, am I ?"

There was a terrific expression of fear and
ferocity in Overbury's countenance, while
mine host was speaking. He had the awe upon
him of listening to one, whom he almost con-

sidered, despite appearances, as addressing
him in accents from the tomb; and he was
surrounded by others, whose presence at that
moment inspired a similar belief of their
spectral character. There were those, too,
before whom he felt that he now stood in all
the hideous nakedness of his hitherto concealed crimes. But, amid all these feelings,
he was not slow to suspect that Wintour might
perhaps be gibing at him, upon the subject of
the trick, which he still considered had been
played him, when he was locked in the Abbey.
Darting therefore a fierce look at mine host,
while his quivering lip betrayed emotions of a
far different character, he exclaimed—

" I am not hunted down yet; though that
thing of hell, Fitz-Maurice, cried havoc ! and
let loose all his fiends to harry me. Then beware ! for what that devilish magician could
not do, 'twill be perilous for such a gad-fly as
yourself to attempt."

Wintour made no reply. His homely wits,

indeed, were so scared by what he saw, and what he saw so entirely engrossed the few thoughts he could call his own, that Overbury's menace, if it reached his ears, certainly found no entrance there to his mind.

" It would be mercy," said Peverell, rising from his seat, " to leave that noble heart in its death-like slumber; for when it wakes, a grief wakes with it, that will pull at its strings till they break. But it may not be ! Mine office is decreed ; and must be fulfilled."

So saying, he advanced with a slow and feeble step towards the further end of the table, where Lacy was sitting, in the same attitude, and with the same aspect, which they all wore when Peverell first looked upon them. He laid his hand upon his shoulder, and in a voice, which had recovered much of its wonted firmness, he exclaimed, in the words of comfort which had descended upon his own troubled spirit, " Benjamin Lacy ! thou gallant soldier !

"Look, up and see
Silent friends who look on thee!"

The spell-bound veteran, released from the
charm that had held all his faculties of mind
and body suspended, covered his eyes with his
hand for a moment; and then, looking earnestly
at Peverell, he said, "You saw it all! Where
is my daughter? where is Helen? and where
is Fitz-Maurice?"

Before Peverell could reply, strains of solemn music were heard. The Abbey shone with
a pale, silvery light, through which its grey
stone walls, and ponderous arches, seemed to
rear themselves in larger bulk, like rocky
heights half obscured by mist; while a trans-
parent vapour, curling away in purple wreaths
from the altar, discovered the forms of Helen
Lacy and Fitz-Maurice! Helen was sitting, as
Peverell had last seen her, gazing wistfully at
that signet, which had married her to idiotcy;
and her ashy features were overspread with a
cold, melancholy smile, like a fair region, in its

pride of summer, despoiled of its loveliness by
the sudden coming of a wintry storm. Fitz-
Maurice stood by her side ; but he was no
longer clothed in his sable vestments, His
flowing mantle, and his towering plume, were
exchanged for the bright armour of a steei-
clad Knight of The Cross, with his mail of
chain, his gauntlets, his pavache shield, his
casque, and mighty two-hand sword. Suspended from a crimson baldrick, of costly
texture, was that holy emblem of our Saviour's
crucifixion, which Peverell had taken from the
altar, and placed within his hands. He looked
at Helen, and his countenance brightened with
a fervent expression of mingled piety, gratitude, and joy.

Familiar as they had all been with scenes of
surpassing wonder, there was something so
calm, so holy, so celestial in this, that they
gazed upon it in silent ec tasy. Lacy deemed
it but a vision ; and the tears trickled down his
cheeks, as he beheld what he believed to be the

shadowy semblance, only, of his for ever lost
child.   Overbury looked at Fitz-Maurice, and
the very chair he sat on shook beneath the
trembling of his body.

The strains of aërial melody ceased.   The
silvery light deepened into a brighter radiance.

" Approach !" exclaimed Fitz-Maurice.

All, except Overbury, advanced slowly towards the altar.   He attempted to rise, but
his limbs denied him their support.   Lacy
leaned, with a tottering step, upon the arm of
Peverell.

" The crowning moment of my triumph,"
said Fitz-Maurice,—" the last and best reward
of all, is at hand.   Forbear !" he continued,
addressing himself to Lacy, whom he perceived
about to rush into the arms of his daughter.
" A gentler course shall dry those tears, old
man, and make thee again a happy father.
Helen Lacy !   Behold—she hears not me.
Oh ! but there is a voice—that voice which
blessed her, many a time and oft, a nursling in

her mother's arms—that voice, which never since hath fallen upon her ear, save in the quickening accents of a self-begetting love, of an unchanged and unchangeable tenderness—let but that sacred voice reach her, and, from the inmost depth of her now blighted heart, she will answer it in gladness !"

Lacy drew nearer to his daughter. In a low faltering tone, he pronounced her name.

Helen looked up. It was beautiful, to see how returning thought and consciousness gradually chased, from her pale features, and from her dull dark eyes, the vacant smile, and the fixed unmeaning stare ; and how their wonted energy and expression stole perceptibly over her countenance, lighting it up with the character of intellectual life, even as a pleasant landscape unveils itself to the sight, when the blue mists of an autumnal morning, covering the earth like an out-spread mantle of sleeping waters, melt away in the beams of the rising sun.

At length, she recognised Lacy ; and then,

with one wild, piercing scream, she started up.
" Father ! Father !" was all she said, as she
flung her arms round his neck, in a paroxysm
of delirious joy, and found sweet consolation in
weeping upon his bosom !

CHAPTER XIII.

A FEW moments were allowed for the indul-
gence of nature's holiest emotions; when Fitz-
Maurice leading the way, they all returned to
the table, filled if possible with feelings of
amazement, greater than had been excited by
any of the preceding incidents in this marvellous drama. It is certain, at least, that,
individually, those feelings were more intense,
except in the case of Wilkins; because, as
regarded all the rest, there were circumstances
of unexplained, and seemingly of inexplicable

mystery, which were multiplied, at each remove from the trance of Clayton, till they
reached their climax in the trials that Peverell
had singly undergone. What next might
happen, scarcely found a place in their thoughts,
so entirely were their minds overwhelmed by
what had happened. They took their seats in
silence, Helen Lacy clinging to her father for
support and protection, and surveying with
quick glances of her still dewy eyes, the martial
figure of Fitz-Maurice, who stood by her side.
His noble port, and his now warrior-like appearance; his glittering armour, which flashed in
radiance from its polished surface, at every
movement of his body; and the serene expression of a great triumph, which dwelt upon his
countenance, were finely contrasted with the
plainer habiliments, and the more anxious features, of those who were gazing at him.

" It were strange," said he, after a lengthened
pause, " if the conflict with yourselves were
other than I see it in your looks. On every

tongue there are a thousand questions, ready for utterance—in every eye there dwells an impatient spirit, eager to be answered. Each of ye, save you, Marmaduke Peverell, and you, Helen Lacy, hath passed through the valley of the shadow of death! Doth this amaze ye? It may amaze thee more to learn, that this heroical maiden, and that undaunted man, inspired of Heaven—for earthly promptings had been too weak—have been to ye angels of life, conducting ye back to this fair world, and to the blessed light of day. Oh, my friends! You may remember with what vehement earnestness, by what solemn injunctions, I implored you to go on, when once you had begun,—and how that earnestness, and those injunctions, grew more vehement, became more solemn, at each step you took. More than then I did, my dark destiny forbad. But you had faith, and you are rewarded! What hath been your reward— what your faith hath done for yourselves, and for me—what my fate must have remained, and what yours must have become, fainting in your trials, prepare to know. My promise was given to him, with whom I first communed, in the unravelling of this great mystery ; and it hath been renewed to yourselves. It shall be redeemed. —Listen, while I reveal wonders ! Listen, but question me not, while, with a fearful spirit, I invoke the memory of the past. It will be yours to discourse with one another of what I tell, when I shall no longer be among you." He paused for a moment ; and then continued :

" I HAVE LIVED THREE HUNDRED YEARS ! In that time—in all that time, I have never seen the glorious sun descend, but followed still its rolling course through the regions of illimitable space. I have shivered on the frozen mountains of the icy north, and fainted beneath the sultry skies of the blazing east : the swift winds have been my viewless chariot, and on their careering wings I have been hurried from clime to clime. But, nor light, nor air, no heat, nor cold, have been to me as to the rest of my species; for I was doomed to find in their extremes a perpetual torment. I howled, under the hsarp, pinching pangs of the icy north; I panted with agony, in the scorching fervour of the blazing east; and when mine eyes have ached, with vain efforts, to pierce the darkness of the earth's centre, they have been suddenly blasted with excessive and intolerable light.

"All the currents of human affection—all, that makes the past delightful, the present lovely, and the future coveted, were dried up within me. My heart was like the sands of the desert, parched and barren. No living stream of hope, of gladness, or of desire, quickened it with human sympathies. It was a bleak and withered region, the fit abode of ever-during sorrow and comfortless despair. I was as a blighted tree, that perishes not at the root, but is withered in all its branches. Tears, I had none. One gracious drop, falling from my seared orbs, would have been the blessed channel of pent-up griefs that seemed to crush my almost frenzied brain. Sighs, I breathed not. They would have heaved from my bursting heart some of that misery, which loaded it to anguish. Sleep never came. I was denied the common luxury of the common wretched, to lose, in its sweet oblivion, its brief forgetfulness, the sense of what I was. Death, natural death, closed his many doors against me. All that lived, except myself,—the persecuted, the weary, and the heavily laden of man's race,— could find a grave! I, alone, looked upon the earth, and felt that it had no resting place for me! God! God! what a forlorn and miserable creature is man, when, in his affliction, he cannot say to the worm, I shall be your's! I might have cast away, indeed, the YENARKON— the Giver of Life—the elixir of the Sibyl—but that would have been to subject myself to a power of darkness, in whose fell wrath I should have suffered the casting away of mine eternal soul!

"Thus the stream of time rolled on, burying beneath its dark waves, our little span of present, in the huge ocean of a perpetual past, and devouring, as the food of both, our swift decaying future. But I floated on its surface, and beheld whole generations flourish and fade away, while age and silver hairs, growing infirmities, and the closing sigh that ends them all, mocked me with a horrible exemption. I remained, and might have remained, for ages yet to come, the fixed and unaltered image of what I was, when in Mauritania I encountered the potent Amaimon, the damned magician of the den, but for that—woman's faith, and man's fidelity—which have made me what I AM!

"This *was* my destiny. Now mark, how I became enthralled to it; and how it befel, that at last I shook it off, and found redemption.

"In my middle manhood, when scarcely forty summers had glowed within my veins, I left my native Italy, and journeyed to the Holy Land, upon the strict vow of a self-im-

posed penance. It was for no sin committed
in my days of youth, but for the satisfaction of
an ardent piety, and the growing spirit of a
long enkindled devotion. I had patrimonial
wealth in Apulia ; I had kindred ; I had
friends. I renounced them all, to dedicate
myself, thenceforth, to the service of THE
CROSS. My purpose was blessed, by a virtuous
mother's prayers, that I might approve myself
a worthy soldier of Christ; and it was sanctified by a holy priest at the altar.

" Even now, the recollection is strong within
me, of the feelings with which, as the rising sun
illumined the tops of the surrounding hills, I
approached the once glorious, and still sacred,
city of Jerusalem—that chosen seat of the
Godhead—that Queen among the nations.
Eclipsed, though it was, and its majestic head
trodden into the dust, by the foot of the infidel,
my gladdened eyes dwelt upon what was im-
perishable, and my rapt imagination pictured
what was destroyed. The vallies of Jehosaphat

and Gehinnon, Mount Calvary, Mount Zion, and Mount Acra, stretched before me. The palace of King Herod, with its sumptuous halls of marble and of gold—the gorgeous Temple of Solomon—the lofty towers of Phaseolus and Mariamne—the palace of the Maccabees—the Hippodrome—the houses of many of the prophets—grew into existence again, beneath the creative force of fancy. I stood and wept. I knelt, and kissed the consecrated earth which once a Saviour trod.

" I fulfilled my vow. Within a month, I became a soldier of Christ. I was ordained a Knight of the Holy Sepulchre.—I knelt before the entrance of the tomb.—I swore the oath of loyalty, of virtue and of valour—of piety, of hospitality, and of the redemption of captives— and I held within my hands the sword of the renowned Godfrey of Boulogne.

" Thus appointed, I longed to signalise my zeal, and I craved some enterprise of great peril, befitting the high calling to which I had devoted myself. Then it was, I learned that three hundred years before, a precious relic had been purloined from the Temple of the Sepulchre : yea, even from that part of it, at the eastern end, beneath the spacious arched concave, which marks the hallowed place whereon our Saviour suffered. Hence, in an evil hour, was stolen, by a sacrilegious caitiff, who knelt in seeming adoration before it, while penitential groans burst from his dissembling heart, the crucifix, vouched by the sacred tradition of ages, as being wrought by holy hands, from the wood of that which the pious Empress Helena caused to be revealed, where it had lain buried for three centuries; and whose identity, as the true cross, she had verified, in curing, by the touch thereof, a noble lady of Jerusalem afflicted with a grievous malady.

" For many years it was believed that the spoiler had bereaved the Temple of the Sepulchre of its gem, only to enrich some other shrine; but at length it was disclosed, in a dream to Gaudentius, then Bishop of Jerusalem, and a man of rare sanctity, that the holy relic had been taken by the dark spirit AMAIMON, who stole into the sanctuary in pilgrim's weeds, and bore it away. He alone, of all the fiends that roam over this fair earth, had power to subdue its influence, and arm himself against it. He alone could couple the miracles of Heaven, with the potent spells of the lower world. His mother was an enchantress; and she had given him skill to touch, unarmed, that from which every other slave of hell flees howling. Possessed of this prize, he triumphed in such arts by its aid, as made him the scourge of the human race. He prowled from region to region, infected every kingdom with his presence, and walked the universal world, a grim monarch, whose path might be tracked by blood and pestilence, by famine, death and horror.

" Each knight of the Holy Sepulchre, at the time of being ordained such, was told, after taking the oath which bound him to the performance of manifold Christian duties, that there remained ONE, to be attempted only by an undaunted follower of the Cross, and to be disclosed, only to those who should first swear to undertake it. Many a gallant heart quitted Jerusalem, sworn to return with the crucifix redeemed, or perish in the enterprise. Alas! they were permitted to accomplish only the latter condition; and even, as I told *thee*, Marmaduke Peverell, when first we held discourse together, their bones whitened the ground in front of the cave, and their flesh fattened the monster which guarded its mouth.

" I eagerly coveted this unknown peril, whose very mystery fired my imagination; and when it was no longer unknown, I coveted it the more. I went through the prescribed ceremonies; knelt before the altar of the holy cross, clothed in a long loose garment, holding in my hand a taper of white wax; in the name of the Father, the Son, and the Holy Ghost, I received my sword—was solemnly girt with a belt—had my spurs fastened on—took the sacrament, and repeated daily, from one lunar crescent, till another appeared in the heavens, a hundred and fifty paternosters, for such as had been already slain in this new crusade.

" It chanced that, in my youth, I knew a famous exorcist. You may remember how I charactered him that night I sat with you here, and spoke not, till a vision that amazed you all had passed away. He was, as then I told you, one who wrought subtle charms, but ever for benign purposes: one who, by his powerful art, could confound the fiends of the lower world when they infected this. He had taught me much; but all I knew from him, or by silent study of my own, equalled not a tithe of his wondrous skill. His name, BARBAZON—his abode, a little rocky island, near to Lesbos. I quitted Jerusalem; embarked on board an argosy of Venice; and ere the sun had three times sunk beneath the western wave, I sat at the feet of the venerable seer, beneath the shade of the olive and the fig-trees which over-arched the entrance to his cave.

" When he learned my errand, his brow darkened with prophetic sorrow. Potent as he was, Amaimon confessed not his power; nor the power of any single spell or charm that he could command. But the good old man applauded my resolve; and the silver moon was high in the heavens, attended by a countless host of glittering stars, ere I ceased to listen to his thrilling words. He bade me stay with him while he should consult his books, commune with himself, and, by necromantic lore, unfold each circumstance that could or thwart or speed, accomplish or defeat, my enterprise.

"I consented; and on the seventh day he led me forth, one morning, to a sequestered corner of the isle, where, in the dim light of a thick myrtle grove, he imparted to me the fruit of his occult labours.

" ' I cannot,' said he, ' assure you of a pros-

perous issue. Amaimon has a triple existence.   He lives, while a monster who guards
his den, by night and by day, and which has
been engendered by his own unhallowed skill,
cannot be destroyed—he lives, while the talisman that he ever wears next his heart, is un-
broken ;—and he lives, while the crucifix you
seek remains in his possession.   But the power
he now exercises is held upon conditions that
are bound up in the preservation of his three-
fold life.   The monster destroyed, and it is
sorely maimed—the talisman broken, and it is
further crippled—the cross recovered, and it is
annihilated ! It lies far, far beyond me, far beyond those instruments with which I can permit myself to work, to give you the certain
means of victory.   Nor would you, perchance,
so choose it, if I could ; for it would rob your
enterprise of some of that glory which is
to be won by an undaunted confronting of danger.   My son ! betide what may, your noble
love of peril will not be stinted in its chivalrous

desires. But I *can* arm you, as those who have
gone before you were *not* armed; and in such
way as will assist thy natural intrepidity. Wear
this, (and he placed a golden SIGNET on my finger,) and if *thou* fail to redeem the Cross at first,
it may redeem it for thee at the last. Whene'er
thou wouldst know how, and what other aids
will then be needful, break the seal of this scroll,
and peruse it. Therein is your fate, when that
fate shall be linked with what that signet must
perform to release you from it. But, mark me
well! I command you, destroy them both by
the agency of fire, and never read the one, or
permit the other to be invoked, unless, failing in
your great enterprise, you fall beneath the accursed power of Amaimon; for his SLAVE you
are, though you sorely maim, and though you
further cripple, if you do not ANNIHILATE him!
I have told you, I cannot assure you a prosper-
ous issue; therefore can I not discover, though
I have sought the knowledge thereof with much
toil, whether thou shalt prosper. But mine art

does inform me how thou wilt fare, missing what thou seekest, yet vanquishing what thou mayst. One thing more, and depart at thy pleasure. Either thou wilt perish, and thy bones whiten in the air, as theirs have done, who, like thee, have adventured in this business—or thou wilt destroy the monster and break the talisman; or, finally, thou mayst achieve the conquest of the Cross. If the first, Heaven's will be done!—if the last, renown among men, and a reward, not of this world, await you—but if the second—let not twelve hours roll o'er your head, as you value your soul's health, ere you refuse the treasures of an empire, and accept—which part from never— the seeming modest guerdon of a little ounce of human flesh.'

" He ceased. My deep attention had devoured each word he uttered. But when I would have questioned him, to learn the fate I must tempt, in that failure which would make me Amaimon's SLAVE, he sighed, and bade me seek to know no more. I obeyed. We parted ; and the evening sun beheld me again upon the waters in quest of this thrice defended necromancer.

" What befel me in Mauritania, thou knowest : at the least, so much as I could *then* tell, and shaped with such circumstances as I was *then* constrained to employ. Even at this distance of time, memory retraces the fierce vicissitudes, and the more than mortal agony, of that dread encounter with a trembling hand. I slew the monster ; I grappled with Amaimon in his den ; I tore the talisman from his heart ; I threw his pestiferous carcass to the earth, a black and strangled corse : but again his spirit was incarnate ; and he re-appeared before me, in that same form he wore when he disputed with me this night, inch by inch, my entrance here. He held the crucifix aloft as then he did : I rushed upon him ; but with the scream of the famished eagle, when it stoops to pounce upon its prey, he exclaimed, ' SLAVE ! I mark

thee for my own !' The fiery blow was given
—the burning impress was there—my brain
was as if all Etna's flames consumed it ; my
eyes grew blind ; I groped in vain to find
Amaimon, and, when my vision returned, I was
alone !

" I knew, in the bitterness of my own soul,
what I had FAILED to do. But I had done a
deed of service in the public eye, and I told
you — Marmaduke Peverell — what mighty
wealth, what wondrous riches I had earned.
I told you, too, how I refused them all, and
how I only claimed and obtained the prophetic
Sibyl's elixir—the Yenarkon—the Giver of
Life—the ' little ounce of human flesh,' which
Barbazon, with fore-knowledge of its use, had
admonished me to ask.

" The twelfth hour came, and then I knew
my doom. Amaimon stood before me. I
FELT his presence—I FELT he glared upon me
—I FELT he breathed upon me—I FELT his
power, like the ambient air, surrounding me,

and pervading my whole frame. The very marrow in my bones confessed the searching poison. I was conscious, intuitively and instinctively, that I had become his SLAVE— that he could command me—that he could dispose of me—and that I was helpless. His look—but I need not describe *that :* you have not forgotten, you never can forget what it was, as your intrepid hand took the cross from the altar, and placed it in mine. Such it was, when now he first surveyed, in his SINGLE being, him who had brought him to it—him, who had for ever destroyed two of the links his devilish art had forged, to hold him to a world he ravaged and deformed.

" I heard my curse: it was brief and terrible. ' The lives thou hast taken, keep ! they are yours. Groan beneath their bondage ! I snap in twain the mingled yarn of mortal existence, which stretches from the cradle to the grave. In the deep earth, nor in the rolling sea, shalt thou find a grave. Slave of my

power, be slave of my slave ! Behold ! the
shadow follows not the substance more closely,
than this thing shall be upon thy steps, to vex,
torment, and harry thee !'

" It was then I saw MEPHOSTO, a filthy and
malignant spirit, the abhorred fruit of a
Moorish vampire, and a hag of Thessaly, whom
Amaimon clothed in youthful beauty, and
made prolific ; while, ere her foul burthen was
ripe within her, she in a trance did cast it
forth. He croaked a demon's fierce delight as
he crawled towards me, and, touching the hem
of my garment, exclaimed—' OBEY !'

" From that moment began my captivity.
From that moment, till this night of my
release at the altar, I endured a bondage such
as I have described ; a bondage, the chains of
which, though I ceaseless strove to break, I
had long despaired of doing ; so cunningly
were they wound about me, and so impossible
of achievement seemed the conditions of my
redemption. Judge what hope could be ex-

tracted from the task assigned me. I found a
time to peruse the sealed scroll of Barbazon."

Fitz-Maurice drew forth a roll of parchment,
and read from it. " This," said he, " was

THE ORACLE.

' When an idiot shall die,
And a mother's heart breaks :
When an idiot shall live,
Who a father's life takes :
When the friend slays the friend ;
And the first is the last,
He takes up the cross,
And thy sorrows are past.'

" And this," he continued, " was its dis-
maying interpretation, in

THE SCROLL.

" 'Thou art now Amaimon's SLAVE, and must
ever be so, till thou shalt find the means to
fulfil the decree of the oracle, which thus I
expound to thee :

" ' In some region of the globe, but place

and time are hidden from me, thou must find
the number of the Apostles—nor more, nor
less—who, of their own free choice, shall be
brought together, to inquire of a great mystery,
by thee made manifest according to thy will.

‘ ‘ When twelve are found, uninfluenced, save
by their several humours, to know the causes
of what they shall see or hear, they are sub-
jected to *your* influence; but in whatsoe'er
thou sayst to them, thou must disclose nor
thyself—nor thy destiny—nor thine aim. Be
towards them as man to man, and reach their
wills by human instruments alone. Persuade,
but command not; assume the oracle in thy
responses, but only to sway their passions.
Work wonders; but let not the wonder-working
hand be visible. So shalt thou in the end,
perchance, work out thy deliverance.

“ ‘ For, if thou shalt thus be able to nerve
their hearts and minds, against all the assaults
of Amamion's potent charms, thou art in the
path of redemption. But thy task is nathless,

full fraught with great and manifold difficulties. Amaimon's power will cross thee at every step. He will blast their eyes and ears with sights and sounds of unutterable woe and horror. He will surround them with such appalling visions, and strike at their fears with such quick-coming terrors, as mortal spirits shall hardly have strength to cope with. Each time, too, that thou defiest him, he shall demand a life, which thou must grant, or forthwith abjure thy struggle with him, and remain his slave; or cast away the Yenarkon, and perish beneath his wrath. But though he can demand a life, and thou must grant one, the death of nature shall not follow, unless final defeat baffle thee; for in *thy* defeat will lie the ratifying sentence of *their* doom; till which they shall be but as sleeping images of death. When Amaimon perishes, all the sacrificed, by whose unforced immolation thou wilt have achieved his perdition, are thereby ransomed from his dark dominion. Heed well, my son, this con-

dition of thy redemption, that thou mayst be
worthy of thy redemption. Let not the blood
of thy fellow man, like the inheritance of the
prodigal, be cast to the winds ; lest the waters
of bitterness flow in upon thee, in the day of
thy triumph. The manner of the sacrifice, too,
lies with thee; as do the occasion, and the
necessity ; forasmuch, that if but one only of
the mystic number faint, and doth forswear the
ordeal, thou art constrained to renounce the
rest, and in another region seek another number
of the apostles.

" ' And it must fall out, that he, whoe'er he
be, that is the *first* impelled to question the
great mystery, shall nor flinch, nor waver, nor
misdoubt himself even to the *last :* for by such
a one, and such only, canst thou *at* the last,
achieve the LAST. It is he, who must take up
the cross, when Amaimon is COMPELLED to lay
it down, which he shall never be, till the other
eleven have braved him to the death. Yea !

and he shall have power to take it again himself, if there be one sun rise ere it is removed.

" ' My son! the tangled thread of thy destiny is not yet unravelled. There must be an idiot's death, and a mother's broken heart. There must be an idiot living, and a dying father's sentence pronounced by the innocent lips of an adoring daughter; and there must be a slaughtered friend, loved by the friend who slays him. In no page can I read — by no communings with the world of spirits can I learn—by no lore I am master of, can I unfold, how these shall come to pass. I only know they are demanded of thee; and thou, foreknowing, must accomplish them. The signet thou wearest will bested thee much. It hath a mighty virtue; and is endued, as thou shalt prove, with wonderous qualities, while worn by thee. Parted from, it hath but THREE. It may command, ONCE, the spirit of the future; it may command, ONCE, the slave that commands thee; it may command, ONCE, Amaimon

himself, when the Cross trembles in his grasp.
And then—it is dross !

" ' Soldier of the holy sepulchre ! Champion
of the Cross ! Wrestle with the powers of
darkness, and return triumphant to Jerusalem !'

" I read and trembled. My doom was fixed.
Despair took possession of me. It was not
within human means to perform what I was
enjoined, and yet *by* human means alone was
I permitted visibly to work ; while Amaimon
might league all hell against me. My spirit
drooped ; hope forsook me. I was hourly on
the rack, beneath the subtle malice of Mephosto;
in whose refined torments I suffered all that a
legion of fiends could have inflicted upon me ;
and often was I tempted, in desperation, to bid
come the worst, by casting from me the Yenarkon. But a higher power, unseen, directed me.
I groaned—I smote my breast—I gnashed my
teeth in agony—but I LIVED !

" Three hundred years had thus rolled on,
and I had suffered a million in anguish ; for

every moment was a year, reckoned by my torture. During that time I essayed, in vain, to discharge me of my task. In Africa, in Asia, on the shores of the Ganges, in the new found world, in Europe, in my native Italy, in Greece, in Spain, in the frozen regions of the Laplander, the Dane, the Norweyan, the Swede, and the Muscovite, in the sunny plains and vallies of France, and in the mountains of Hungary, I sought the means of challenging Amaimon. Whithersoever he went, there followed I, and wrought my mysteries; as various in their character and outward shew, as were the scene of each, and the people whose wonder I was to move. But there was ever some link wanting; ever some circumstance that failed me; some accursed chasm, which left me to the scorn and mockery of Amaimon —to the avenging torments of Mephosto.

"At length the realm of proud and mighty England confessed his presence, and became my theatre. And there I found a Marmaduke

M 3

Peverell, and a Helen Lacy! I know not why, but when first I looked upon this ocean queen —when first I surveyed her populous cities and her verdant plains—when first I breathed the air that freemen breathed, I felt as if it, or none, were the soil that was to give me freedom. How I have sped, this blessed moment best may tell.

"I selected St. Albans. Why? Because I had the power to know, that herein dwelt an idiot girl, a doating mother's much loved treasure. I had never before had my enterprise so auspicated. To my mind, she was the hostage for the rest; the good and sure omen of what was to follow. I wrought my mystery. But two successive nights, the charmed fire curled round these walls, and shot through these dim windows in vain. I watched: no footstep came. The third, and if I failed, the last, I observed, unseen, you, Marmaduke Peverell, and your well-beloved friend, who now sits beside thee. I noted the cool, determined spirit,

with which you rode up to the door, and *satisfied* yourself; and hope beat high within me.
The next night came. I filled the hearts of
hundreds with wondering terror. That night,
the idiot girl perished! And thus was un-
twisted one thread in the tangled skein of my
destiny.

" Amaimon, on the following day, appeared
among your townspeople, who were met to deli-
berate what it was fitting, or best to do, touching the mystery of the over night. Fain would
he have crushed at once the rising spirit I
had kindled ; and when that honest fanatic, Kit
Barnes, avowed himself ready to 'pass the
Abbey doors ere the clock struck twelve, and
abide the rest,' Amaimon laid his demon hand
upon him, breathing words of fire into his ears,
that he might be staggered in his intents. I
was passive here. Save that my thoughts were
upon you, Marmaduke Peverell, I would not
have used the signet's power to make Mephosto
lacquey me, in freedom, while the evening star

performed its bidden motions thrice round the
moon.

"Midnight came. Amaimon arrayed himself in terror. Kit Barnes entered the Abbey,
and you, (still addressing Peverell) calm and
unruffled, stood without. You approached the
door, and would have struck upon it. 'Twas
I who made powerless your arm, and pronounced the words, *Thou fool, why so impatient ? Thou art the last !* With a prophetic
spirit, I had now marked you for the *last*, and
I put your firmness to its test.

"Kit Barnes came forth. You inquired what
had taken place. His answer was, *I am forbidden to tell !* Amaimon had wrought a vision
here, darkly prophesying of that which must
happen, if another, and another, and another
night followed, mingled with such augmenting
circumstances of horror, as had already, many
a time and oft, been my bane. Then, breathing
into his nostrils a withering poison which
curdled the ruddy stream of life, he left him to

die, when next the hour of midnight sounded
in his ears. His lips he sealed in silence, to
strike that terror which unrevealed danger doth
ever breed, from the fancy's aptitude to coin
what is most dreadful in what is most unknown.

" Chance did for me what it had never done
before. Chance, shall I call it ?—No ! It was
the will of Heaven that I should here, at last,
find the apostolic number. Twelve assembled
within these walls.—Oh ! as I sat, in silent
agony, and looked upon you all that night, my
spirit wept to think how you might fare, if I
fared ill ; how near was your doom, if the end
of mine were still to elude me. But you were
spared that pang which wrings our nature most,
when, full of life we make sad preparation for
the grave. You knew not your peril ; and to
die, being the tenure by which we live, to die
only once, is a quittance upon easy terms, when
we consider how many deaths there are to many,
in the expectation of that once.

" Amaimon worked with all his power, for

he feared the intrepid band that was now op-
posed to him.   The effeminate Italian, the
luxurious Asiatic, the volatile Frenchman, the
phlegmatic German, the brute savage of the
desert, and the barbarian infidel of the crescent,
had confessed the mighty influence of his arts.
But the cool, fearless, reasoning Englishman,
who looks at danger with a prudent forethought
how best he may leap the space between, then
grapple, and after, never think of it—he had
now to scare with the novelty of terror.   He
knew this, I say, and he worked with all
his power.   I was with you, but could cross
him only in the beginning, and in the end.   I
diffused that balmy, roseate atmosphere, which
dissolved your senses in the languor of luxurious
repose.

"Knowing what now you do, you may imagine, better than I can describe, how my bosom
swelled with increasing hope, when, as we were
about to quit the Abbey, we were encountered
by that grief-crazed woman, the mother of the

idiot girl. They only, if there were any such, who had endured for an hour what I had for myriads of hours—they only who could feel what I felt, at the glimmer of a mere possibility that the moment of my release was at hand, can judge me when I say, my spirits staggered under the sudden rush of joy produced by those few words she pronounced in so sad a tone— ' *My heart is breaking, hour by hour!*' I heeded not her tale of the dead man's dying throes —nor of his frantic visions—Amaimon's work. I heard only her deep lamentations for her lost child—I saw only her haggard misery—and I thought only of the first of my required tasks:

" ' When an idiot shall die,'
And a *mother's heart breaks.*'

" This would be the confession of a demon, were it not mine—the SLAVE of a demon, the price of whose liberty was to be paid down in these tears and in this innocent blood !

" Amaimon crouched beneath the recoil of

his power that night, and trembled. I knew it, from the auxiliaries he employed : for, with his own hand, he anointed mine eyes with the blinding juice of a drug bestowed upon him by his mother, and the secret of whose composition died with that enchantress. The effect of this unguent was, that for four-and-twenty hours, if I looked upon a mortal face, my visual orbs would melt away, as the icicle dissolves, in the warm sun-beam.

" Hence I came not on the following night : but then it was I reaped the full harvest of Barbazon's prescient care. I summoned to my presence my faithful NAPHTAL, the Attendant Spirit of the Signet—communed with him—and swifter than a falling star shoots athwart the heavens, he left me to perform my bidding. I had commanded you to watch for signs — for I knew not what spell of Amaimon might keep *me* from you, though none could control the signet. *Naphtal* was Fortescue—the bearer of that packet, whose oracular lines were so aptly

divined ; and of that letter whose mystic import was no less shrewdly gathered, in all that
appertained to its immediate intendment. Its
first was for the time. Its last, *for* the last.
' *He that hath faith, shall have it.*' You all
had faith in me, and you have all received faith
from me. ' *I come not, but there shall be* MANY
the better, when there is ONE.' You, Marmaduke Peverell, were the last—You were *the*
ONE, and ALL live again, because yours was the
consummating act of my ransom.

"My faithful Naphtal did me noble service.
He returned with tidings of this perfect and
exalted creature—Helen Lacy ;—and of all the
secret workings of her filial love. I saw, at once,
the bright link that united her with my destiny.
I read, as in a volume opened before me, the
page which no lore that Barbazon was master of,
could unfold. A conscious presage dwelt upon
my spirit, that it was on this fair hand the signet, after having discharged itself of its triple
quality, should become dross. A warning

voice within me proclaimed the coming triumph
In all the past, I had never seen (nor had the
knowledge thereof been imparted) a being surrounded with such circumstance to light the
torch of hope, as was this incomparable maiden !
And therefore, never till then, did Naphtal
supplicate so eagerly, that he should work his
own will, by the power he obeyed. For the
first time, since Barbazon placed it on my hand,
the signet was parted from ; and I prepared to
watch or shape the events that were to call forth
its THREE COMMANDS.

" The meteors that flash in sudden radiance
across a troubled sky, taking each moment
new and fantastic shapes, may hardly compare
with Naphtal, nimbly to assume what form
soever, of living nature or of dead, of man,
or of brute, or of inert substance, which the
errand he would compass might demand. He
it was who lured you (addressing Peverell), in
your morning walk, to where, an instant after,
he deftly lay before you, the image of a mur-

dered man—of that Fortescue, upon whom you found the bridal gift of Helen Lacy's mother, which, with like dextrous speed, he had thither brought from the hovel of the sorceress. The hag, Margery Ashwell, was powerful and willing. But her skill, unaided by Naphtal, had been all too little to work my issues. By him instructed, and by him provided, when this maiden sought her, both first and last, she unravelled another of the tangled threads that bound me Amaimon's slave."

Fitz-Maurice paused for a moment: then, bending his eyes upon Helen, whose countenance shewed that she was under the same fascination while listening to him, as when her ears first drank the thrilling tones of his voice, he addressed her, in accents, tremulous with emotion, yet deep and solemn in their pathos, as he thus continued.

" It was glorious to behold how delicately Naphtal wove the web that enmeshed thee ; how daintily he surrounded you, with apt devices, now a dream—now a harper's minstrelsy—and now a glittering miracle—such as best might sway thy flexile fancy. In parting with that SIGNET, I surrendered to him the power and right to use what means and contrivances his own subtle spirit might devise to place it on thy hand, so that, in the fulness of time, thou mightest aid in striking off my fetters. How *he* sped, is told in how *I* have triumphed!

" Mine was the task, to awaken in thy gentle bosom those natural solicitations to thy will, which might incline it to act in a pre-ordained path with seeming freedom. The chord that vibrated deepest in thy heart, was filial affection. It was that I touched. But, as the sun is the source of universal light through all creation, so is the holy love that kindles for a parent, the source of every virtue that descends upon our kind. I had but to plead for pity, as a very wretch who had drained his cup of misery to the dregs, and sighs, and tears were the gracious harbingers of my successful suit. A father's weal was still the *first*—but it was no longer the ONLY object of thy prayers !"

A faint flush crimsoned the face of Helen as Fitz-Maurice uttered the last words. Her humid eyes had met the fond gaze of her father, while Fitz-Maurice spoke of the " chord that vibrated deepest in her heart ;" but she listened, with intense earnestness, to his recital of the means by which she had been wrought upon to perform her part in his deliverance. He now addressed them collectively again.

" After the second night, I found you wavering; and I had to persuade, ' but not command,' to ' assume the oracle ;' to ' work wonders ;' but ' conceal the wonder-working hand.' I did all. My persuasions, my oracular responses—and the liquid scroll within the cross, bound you to four nights more, ere which, I looked to accomplish the ' *friend slaying the friend.*' I was not defeated. The third night, when I was

with you, though Amaimon's spells shrouded
me in darkness, saw the mystic sacrifice of one
who was friend and kinsman conjoined. That
night, too, my trusty Naphtal, in frolicsome
mood, punished the blustering curiosity of your
brace of townsmen, who were fain to be con-
tented with a mystery outside, instead of finding
quick destruction within. Had they not been
so buffeted home to their beds, a fiercer spirit
would have sent them to their graves ; for the
addition of but one beyond the twelve was the
perdition of all.

" Nor was it less the perdition of all if one
of the twelve should ' faint and forswear the
ordeal ;' and hence the seeming fate of him of
The Rose." (Mine host quaked—but said
nothing.) " You," he continued, looking at
Wintour, while a benignant smile beamed
upon his features, as he noted his consternation,
" *you would* have fainted, and played the
recreant, maugre your oath : aye—it was even
so—and I see the confession of it in your looks

—but Naphtal stopped your journey to Dunstable." (The appearance of mine host was now
exceedingly sheepish.) "And how? With me,
lay the ' manner of each sacrifice,' as also ' the
occasion and the necessity ;' and I *could* have
protected myself by a less complex exercise of
my privilege ; but it was Naphtal's delight,
(and I could deny him nothing), to sport with
reverend grey-beards in the robes of office, and
mock dull mortals with their own solemnities.
In Milan once, he walked a seeming criminal to
execution : but when, upon the scaffold, the
headsman thought to smite him with the axe,
he chopped the incorporeal air only, while the
gaping multitude looked on and laughed to see
the malefactor rise and walk away. So it was
his humour, here, to be the Venetian youth, or
gipsy boy, whose father, a shadow like himself,
had died for very want.

"I rejoiced in the power I had, on the fourth
night, to wring a guilty soul !" The countenance of Fitz-Maurice darkened, as he fixed

his eyes sternly upon Overbury, who hung his head, and spoke not. " The desire I had to do so was one motive for my presence ; the perfect means to do so I owed to Helen Lacy's intrepid calling forth of the SIGNET'S SECOND MANDATE. The abhorred Mephosto had thus become, for twelve hours, MY slave ; and it was to torture him, more than he had ever tortured me, to make him work as then I did, *against* Amaimon. But I had another and a greater motive to shew myself that night. HELEN LACY WAS MINE ! I had won from her a troth-plight, which I did not dare to dally with. Moreover, I trembled to protract, by multiplying, the trials of your fidelity. And why did I tremble ? For myself ALONE ? No ! God is my witness, that separate from the feeling which revolved round my own fate, deep and terrible was the one that revolved round the fate of those who were already as ' sleeping images of death !' Sharp and bitter was my torment, lest the fear of the future might come over those that remained, ere the 'perdition of Amaimon should ransom all from his dark dominion.' I wished not the ' blood of my fellow man, like the inheritance of the prodigal, to be cast to the winds.' Therefore it was I swore you to myself last night ; and, therefore, it was, I then defied Amaimon to a banquet of blood this night, which he could not refuse ; but which if he failed to quaff, to the LAST DROP, the cross was within my reach till sun-rise !

" Oh ! how he tormented me the while ! For he knew that I was fast escaping from his fangs, and so resolved to glut himself with vengeance. How, too, he stirred the inmost depths of hell, to arm him for the encounter : to blast each mortal sense with accumulated horrors ! Even I beheld, with inward terror, the visible workings of his power. It was a night to confound all nature, and strike mere man with frenzy.

" But first he sought to shake *your* faith," addressing Peverell, " and craven *your* firm heart, by the smooth imposture of Conrad

Geister. Defeated in that, he arrayed himself
in stupendous might, and wrought the scene
which followed. It was a subtle—a cunningly
contrived one ; so cunningly contrived, that
I threw myself upon my only remaining chance,
that of conjuring each of you to cast not one
look behind. Your fidelity filled me with
amazement. But it was the inspiration of
Heaven that breathed such enduring courage
into your hearts !

" Then came this noble maiden, whose sire,
the ' *eleventh who had braved Amaimon to the
death,*' he grasped on the threshold of the
phantom tomb, to keep from it. The rest had
fallen, one by one, into those shadowy graves,
which worked not their purposed dismay, because it was Naphtal's office to hang a
vapoury cloud around them till the last approached ; and so each, but the last, believed
his danger faced him, and which still he seemed
to escape.

" When," continued Fitz-Maurice, with a
kindling energy of manner, which increased, at

each word, as he spoke, " when ' the innocent lips of an adoring daughter pronounced a father's sentence ;' when ' the cross trembled in Amaimon's hand'—and the THIRD COMMAND of the signet compelled him to relinquish his grasp—when I looked, and saw this incom‑ parable creature, ALIVE, but her reason in eclipse, then it was I knew there only re‑ mained that the 'first,' who, was *now* the 'last,' should 'take up the cross,' which Amai‑ mon had laid, howling, upon the altar, before sun-rise. I did not fear you, Marmaduke Peverell! I did not fear you! Further trials awaited you ; but you had stood the assaults of Amaimon too bravely, to quail now. But what I *did* fear, was his glozing speech ;—the gentle invitation to ask of Conrad Geister, at the twelfth hour, 'to close thine eyes in sleep till sun-rise.' I could not, for I dared not, unmask the device. I approached the altar ! I sounded in your ears your own free oath ! It was enough ! The cross was mine ! I tri‑ umphed !—The unclean spirit perished !"

Fitz-Maurice ceased. He had enjoined
them not to speak, while he invoked the memory of the past; and now, when he was silent,
there was no one among them master enough
of his own thoughts to give them utterance.
Much of what he had said was still a mystery,
which could become intelligible to all, only
when they should be able to confer with each
other. In a few moments he again addressed
them; but his manner was more calm and subdued. The excitement of his feelings had subsided; the deep emotions awakened by his
recital of what he had endured, and by the
exulting consciousness of what he had achieved,
had passed away.

"It is not meet," said he, "that I straight
divest myself of the necromantic power I possess. For thrice three days and nights I must
still employ it before it is renounced for ever,
and all my rest of mortal life spent in holy
penance and devout thanksgiving for this deliverance. Whither I go, shall be made known
to you in due season. Look to find it so, ere

grey hairs come. Peace is now restored to your affrighted town, by the triumph of that which is the emblem of all peace and good-will to man !"

Again he paused. Then, slowly and grace-fully bending on one knee, he took the hand of Helen Lacy, which he pressed respectfully to his lips, exclaiming, in a voice slightly agitated :

" To thee, fair one, a prayer for pardon is earnestly proffered ! Nobly have the daughter and the heroine shone in thy deeds ! The God who hears me, and myself, alone know how I have pitied thee ;—what endured, what offered to endure, that so *thou* mightest have been spared the sharpest of *thy* trials. But it was beyond me ! I have knelt to you, before, in sup-plication, and you granted the boon I asked. I kneel to you now, in gratitude, and you will not refuse the offering. This SIGNET, which I thus remove, is vile and worthless, having dis-charged itself of its wondrous properties ; but here is a gem, (and he placed a matchless chry-solite upon her finger) which Helen Lacy, perhaps, will deign to wear, in poor remembrance of him who must still be to her—Fitz-Maurice !"

He again pressed her hand to his lips, and arose ; while Helen silently bowed her head, in token of acquiescence, without once venturing to lift her eyes towards him.

" The dawn approaches," he continued ; " but no sunrise must greet me within these walls. May they never again be defiled by such abominations as we have seen !"

" Amen to that, with all my heart," responded Clayton, audibly.

" I am no seeker of forbidden things," said Peverell, after a pause, addressing Fitz-Maurice ; " and when I ask you, as now I do, whether we part this hour for aye, you will answer me as it may seem meet to you I should be answered."

" In this world, brave heart," replied Fitz-Maurice, " we meet no more !"

Peverell was silent. No one else spoke. A gentle sigh was breathed by Helen, as Fitz-Maurice, taking each by the hand, bade farewell. He grasped the hands of Peverell and

Lacy (especially the former), with visible emotion. Clayton and mine host manifested somewhat of a coy reluctance, and presented him only with the tips of their fingers, as if they had certain misgivings, in their own minds, touching the propriety of too familiar a contact with so questionable a personage. Fitz-Maurice smiled. As he passed Overbury, who stood sullenly aloof from the rest, he fixed his eyes upon him with a severe and terrible expression.

" I have no hand for thee—no parting word of friendship or of fellowship,—thou man of blood! Hence! And if this world's justice smite thee not, let every hour, yea, every minute, of the days thou art permitted to live, see thee on thy bended knees, seeking mercy and forgiveness from divine justice. Hadst thou as many years, as in thy natural course, thou canst have but moments, before thee, thou mightest well dread they would be all too few, for the atoning penitence that can wash out the deep stains of thy most guilty soul !"

Overbury, callous and reckless, as he had

been, in the knowledge that his crimes were not written upon his brow, for all men to read, felt himself crushed to the very dust, when they were proclaimed aloud; and this solemn appeal to his conscience, which rung in his ears like his death-knell, filled him with awe. It was not till Fitz-Maurice, followed by the rest, had reached the doors of the Abbey, that he seemed to have power to move; and then, suddenly rushing past them, he fled towards his own house, filling the air with blasphemous cries, like a maniac.

When they quitted the Abbey, Mephosto gallopped up, leading by the bridle rein Fitz-Maurice's palfrey. He leaped to the ground, crouched before Fitz-Maurice, and croaked out, " I tarried till the hour, and you came not! At thy mighty bidding am I now come!"

Fitz-Maurice made no reply, but vaulting into his saddle, and waving his hand as he exclaimed, " Once more, farewell, to each and all of ye!" with the speed of an arrow, he and Mephosto vanished from their sight.

CHAPTER XIV.

" I HOLD it good," said De Clare, as they
walked along, after the departure of Fitz-Maurice, " that the wonders we have to discourse of
with each other, pass not our lips, till needful
sleep, and some hours of silent meditation,
string our minds and bodies for the conference.
Such broken and disjointed speech as we now,
perforce, must make, of what we have to impart, would be but like the flashes of a dying
taper thrown upon the coignes and out-jettings
of a storied tapestry, which distort the little

N 3

they darkly show, and leave the perfect whole unrevealed."

" This is certainly no hour for talking," replied Peverell ; "and if it were, I have no tongue for words."

" By Jupiter !" exclaimed Mortimer, " such is not my condition. I have a tongue so overlaid with words, and a brain so crammed with matter waiting impatiently for words to play the midwife and deliver it, that my words and my matter are like two teams wedged in a narrow lane, the more they strive to relieve each other, the faster they stick together."

" I have never discovered," said De Clare, " that there was such a connexion between your tongue and your head, as your similitude implies."

" Nay, an' you talk of similitudes, mark you," added Owen Rees, " what similitude, I pray you, is there between the beginning and the end of these magics ? For look you—"

" Aye," interrupted De Clare, " for look

you!— There are the glimmering streaks of awakening day; and let not its full opening eye stare broadly down upon us, like time-wasters, stealing to our beds at the lag-end of a night revel."

Thus they discoursed; but Lacy, Walwyn, and the others, were too much occupied with their own thoughts to take any part in the conversation, and shortly after, they separated for their several homes.

What was the consternation, (and it must be hoped, the delight) of dame Clayton, when she found she was no widow; what the amazement of mine host, when his arrival at *The Rose* disturbed the black-eyed Lucy in the arms of Tim the ostler, a full hour before her usual time of up-rising; what, his own surprise, to see their terror, and to feel that he was more than half persuaded he had actually been throttled in his bed, instead of riding to Dunstable; and what was the joy, at last, of the good Winifrid Wilkins, to look

again upon her son Walter, though at first,
the shock had nearly made her the thing she
mourned,—all these, and all the grave per-
plexities, of Clayton, mine host, Vehan, and
Wilkins, themselves, before they could discover the right clue to their own mysteries,
must be left to the imagination of the reader.

With regard to the caitiff, Wilfrid Overbury,
his end was as his whole life had been—a stain.
In the frenzy of that guilt which had long tormented him in secret, and beneath whose scor-
pion-lash he now writhed, in its divulged enor-
mity, he flung himself upon his bed.   And oh !
what a hell of torture raged within him !   He
could not hope for longer impunity, even in
this world. The gibbet and the halter reared
themselves before his eyes ; the yells of loathing
thousands sounded in his ears, as he swung, like
a dog, from the scaffold: every artery in his body
throbbed with agony. But it was a crisis of his
fate, for which he had always held himself prepared, desperately resolved never to pay the forfeit

of his crimes, by the hand of the public executioner. A small phial of subtle poison, the knowledge of whose deadly properties he had purchased of a Venetian bravo, and whose fatal virtues he had too often proved in deeds of dark revenge, he ever carried about him. Within an hour after he had quitted the Abbey, he drained its contents; and ere the beams of the morning sun streamed cheerfully through the windows of his chamber, the miserable suicide was beyond the reach of human punishment!

The shadows of evening had begun to fall the next day, when Peverell, De Clare, Mortimer, and all who had been partakers of these mysteries, assembled at the house of Lacy. The recital by Peverell, of what had been his individual share of them, rivetted their attention. Then followed many a surprising tale from the rest, and many a fearful conjecture of what might have happened, if that which did happen had not taken place. The gentle Helen, too, had her miracles and her trials to recount; her

visit to Margery Ashwell; the parting with her
cross; her demanding of the signet from Peverell; her interviews with Fitz-Maurice; her
darkly prophetic dream; and her bridal visit to
the Abbey. The midnight chimes sounded,
ere they had travelled through half the wonders
they had to discourse of; and his worship, the
mayor, whose presence on the occasion had been
duly solicited, could not refrain from " thank-
ing God that matters were as they were, and
that it had not been necessary for him to attend
her majesty's council upon the business."

And thus ended the marvellous history of the
FIVE NIGHTS ! But it was long ere those who
could tell that history, found their task ended
of recounting it to many a stranger who visited
St. Albans, drawn thither by the wide spread-
ing rumour of its miraculous character. Years
glided on, and still the promised communication
from Fitz-Maurice came not, though grey
hairs, and even death, had come to some, to
whom that promise was made. His worship

had lived to a good old age, and closed his eyes in peace, lamenting to the last the supineness of the council, which had neglected to send for him. Wilfrid Overbury's house fell to decay, because, in addition to its being under the ban of blood, in consequence of the murder of Sir Hubert de Falconbridge, the ghost of Overbury himself was seen every stormy night sitting astride the chimney, giving orders to his men as if he was still master of the SCORPION. A black mark, too, continued to be shewn upon the bench at *The Rose*, where Reginald Fortescue had sat ; and the field where his body was found by Peverell, was long after called *The Murder Field ;* while Margery Ashwell was found, one Sabbath morning, hanging in the church porch, with a bible round her neck.

In something less than two years, dame Clayton became safely a disconsolate widow. But she speedily took comfort to herself again, in matrimony ; for she wedded, first, Peter Simcox, the doctor ; secondly, Andrew Grim, the lawyer; and thirdly, a young man, aged twenty, ycleped Mathew Wincup, by trade a carpenter; who married her money at Lammas, and buried herself, come Twelfth Tide following. Little Bridget, too, consented to espouse Andrew Stubbs, and became the fruitful mother of a numerous family of the Stubbs's; while Crab, his worship's serving man, was set up by his master, shortly before his death, as mine host of *The Rose*, John Wintour having removed to the sign of *The Boar* at Leicester. Owen Rees had retired into Wales, upon succeeding to ten acres of patrimonial rock, and seven goats, in his native county of Glamorgan. Mortimer, the gay and silken Mortimer, had betaken himself to the wars, and approved himself a good and valiant soldier, in many a hard-fought field.

Thus time crept on, and changes, such as have been recorded, followed in its ceaseless flow. More than thirteen years had elapsed, and of those who had sat the first night in the

Abbey, seven only continued to reside at St. Albans: Walter Wilkins, Philip Vehan, De Clare, Walwyn, Hoskyns, Lacy, (who was tottering on the edge of the grave, with the gentle Helen for his constant companion,) and Marmaduke Peverell. In all that period, there had been no tidings of Fitz-Maurice. De Clare would sometimes remark, when adverting to his departure on the last night, that " he had disappeared with the speed of an arrow, and, like the arrow, had left no trace, behind, of his course."

It was towards the close of a wintry day, in the middle of December, 1584, that a stranger presented himself at Peverell's door, and inquired for him. He was conducted into his presence, and being seated, forthwith communicated his errand, in such graceful speech, as beseemed his carriage and apparent condition.

" I have no manner of doubt," said he, having ascertained that Peverell's baptismal name was Marmaduke, " that I fulfil my promise in delivering this sealed packet to you. Of its contents," he continued, " I know nothing; but I shall briefly impart how it came into my keeping. I am on my return home, after a journey of three years and more, to Egypt, the Holy Land, and Italy. While at Jerusalem, I sojourned with the Pater Guardian, as he is called, of the monastery of the Franciscans, in that venerable city; a very reverend old man, who, when he learned I was of England, and tending thitherward my vagrant steps, did desire of me, right earnestly, to charge myself with this office. He enjoined me diligently to seek you out, and deliver this into your own hands, adding thereto, that it was from one PIETRO MANFRONI, of Apulia, but then, a holy anchorite, vowed to solitude and prayer. It hath pleased Heaven that I should prosper in mine errand, and that thou shouldst receive into thine own hand, what I now most gladly deliver."

Peverell took the packet. It was folded in

a silken cover, sealed with three seals, suspended by purple ribbons, and directed for " Master Marmaduke Peverell, St. Albans, England."

" I cannot say," said Peverell, after a short pause, and examining attentively the seals, all of which bore the impress of a crucifix, " that I am known to, or have any knowledge of, such a person as you have named. Yet I doubt not, you have rightly sped in your errand; for the trouble whereof, accept my very hearty thanks. May I crave to know your name ?"

" Henry Heicroft," replied the stranger; " and I am speeding with what haste I can to my home, which lieth in Warwickshire. I have been a truant longer by twelve months, than I promised to be, when I set forth upon my journey."

Peverell pressed him to stay the night and refresh; but he would not be persuaded, saying, " Every hour I now lose in England will

be more reproach to me, than all the months
I have added to my absence in foreign coun-
tries." He therefore took his departure, with
much courtesy; and when he was gone, Peverell, with an impatient hand, broke the seals
of the packet. Enclosed within the silken
cover was a letter from Fitz-Maurice, beautifully engrossed upon vellum; which he had
no sooner perused than he forthwith invited to
his house, that same evening, De Clare, Wilkins, Vehan, Hoskyns, Walwyn, Lacy, and
his daughter Helen. He communicated what
had passed between himself and Master Henry
Heicroft, and then read to them the epistle, of
which he had been the bearer. They listened
to it, not without emotion, especially Helen;
for it seemed to them like the last memorial,
except what lingered in their own recollections,
of the wondrous mysteries which had followed
them at every step of their FIVE NIGHTS!

This was the letter:

" *To the Right Noble, and Incomparably Esteemed, Marmaduke Peverell. Pietro Manfroni sends this, from the Holy City, greeting him with much Love and Honour : the Grateful Offering of him, who, in his Bondage, was Fitz=Maurice; who, in his Redemption, is the Servant of God; and who, in his Supplications to Heaven, forgetteth not the Heart and Hand that wrought his Deliverance.*

" The Holy Cross now hangs again in the Sanctuary of the Temple of the Sepulchre; and Pietro Manfroni, the Anchorite of Mount Calvary, never kneels before it, in pious adoration and rapt devotion, without remembering, in his prayers, that Marmaduke Peverell and Helen Lacy ransomed him from bondage : from a bondage which robbed him of the only common birthright of man—the privilege to die!

"Peace be with you, if this find you living! The peace of God be thine, if the grave hath received thee! Once, in every four-and-twenty hours, I sit beside mine own; welcome it as a kind friend I had deemed for ever lost; and await, with humble resignation, but ceaseless hope, my summons to make it my dwelling-place!"

THE END.

SHACKELL AND BAYLIS, JOHNSON'S COURT, LONDON.

Ingram Content Group UK Ltd.
Milton Keynes UK
UKHW020031160323
418612UK00007B/314